FAMOUS
CANADIAN
ACTORS

The Stories Behind Today's Popular Hollywood Celebrities

Stone Wallace

FOLK LORE PUBLISHING

© 2005 by Folklore Publishing
First printed in 2005 10 9 8 7 6 5 4 3 2 1
Printed in Canada

The Publisher: Folklore Publishing

Website: www.folklorepublishing.com

Library and Archives Canada Cataloguing in Publication

Wallace, Stone, 1957–
    Famous Canadian actors : the stories behind today's
    popular Hollywood celebrities / Stone Wallace.

(Great Canadian stories)
Includes bibliographical references.
ISBN 1-894864-43-3

    1. Actors—Canada—Biography. 2. Actresses—Canada—
Biography.
I. Title. II. Series.

PN1998.2.W23 2005   791.43'028'092271   C2005-901819-4

Project Director: Faye Boer
Project Editor: Tom Monto
Production: Trina Koscielnuk
Cover Design: Valentino & Burch

Cover Images: Courtesy of International Communications Systems

Photo Credits: Every effort has been made to accurately credit the sources
of photographs. Any errors or omissions should be directed to the publisher for changes in future editions. Photographs courtesy of International Communications Systems

We acknowledge the support of the Alberta Foundation for the Arts
for our publishing program.

PC: P5

Table of Contents

Dedication

This book is dedicated with love to my beautiful stepdaughter Lauren Cathleen "Peachy" Urbanowich.

Acknowledgements

Once again I would like to thank the fine people at Folklore Publishing for their superior editorial and design work that would make any author proud. Special thanks to Folklore publisher Faye Boer and my editor Tom Monto for their help, support...and patience. Additional thanks must go to Dr. Philip Chamberlin, a true film historian, for supplying the excellent photos that accompany this text. I must thank Dr. Philip's better half, Dolores Fuller, for generously allowing me her office space during my stay in Las Vegas, where this book was written. And a special "thank you" to Tommy Fuller, a whiz kid with computers who frequently got me out of tough technical spots.

Introduction

CANADA HAS PRODUCED SOME EXTRAORDINARY YOUNG actors. Some have become bona fide superstars. Others are respected for their work, but are not as big a draw with the ticket-buying public. Some remain on the rise, while there are those who have already begun to fade from people's memory.

Jim Carrey, Mike Myers, Keanu Reeves and Michael J. Fox firmly represent that first class of actors. Each has attained heights envied by many of their American counterparts. Kiefer Sutherland is a good example of the second category. He consistently delivers strong performances in films, but cannot be regarded as a "superstar." Kim Cattrall is another performer who has enjoyed a solid career, particularly on television, but is not potent box office. Brendan Fraser and Carrie-Anne Moss, despite appearing in many popular movies, still have careers on the rise. Pamela Anderson, on the other hand, has in recent years allowed her popularity to slide. She announced her retirement from acting some time ago, but even before the announcement, her career had entered a slump, unless one counts her popularity with the tabloid press. This is no reflection on Pamela; rather, it's the "flavour of the month" syndrome that has plagued virtually every blonde television actress from Farrah Fawcett to Loni Anderson. The star shines brightly for a time and then begins to fade. Recently, she reported that she has decided to return to acting, so the phoenix may rise again from the ashes.

There is one last category of Canadian actors that should be acknowledged: the veteran actor who has achieved success and recognition and maintains his or her popularity at that level. And who better to exemplify that role than Dan Aykroyd. Dan may not be as young as others featured in this book. He's been well-known to audiences since 1975 when he was one of the original "Not Ready for Prime Time" players on TV's innovative *Saturday Night Live*. But Dan's placement on this list is important. Jim Carrey, Mike Myers and others looked upon him as a mentor—a leader of a new breed of Canadian talent, as Lorne Greene had been for an earlier generation of dramatic actors that included Leslie Nielsen and William Shatner.

The stories behind many of these Canadian successes are fascinating. One of the biggest of today's stars toiled at his craft for years with little reward before achieving stardom, while another was discovered while attending a football game.

These mini-biographies are intended to give the reader insights into the lives of these home-grown celebrities who literally "broke through the border" into international prominence…and did their country proud.

CHAPTER ONE

Jim Carrey
(1962–)

TALL, GANGLY, RUBBER-FACED JIM CARREY IS NOT ONLY THE most popular comic actor in the world, but also the best paid. The entertainment world gasped when this poor kid from Canada was offered a reported $20 million for his work in *The Cable Guy* (1996). But as much as Jim is known for his comedy, he has also shown his ability as a dramatic actor in such films as *The Truman Show* (1998) and *Man on the Moon* (1999). He is a true versatile talent who has overcome the hardships of his youth and disappointments of an early career to become one of the most recognized names (and faces) in show business.

James Eugene Carrey was born to Percy and Kathleen on January 17, 1962, in Newmarket, Ontario. Jim had three older siblings, Pat, John and Rita. The household was not a stable one because their mother suffered from depression and was often chronically sick. Dad Percy, however, had a jovial personality. He had once professionally played the saxophone in a band but was working as an accountant. He never reached his

potential and was reminded of this one day when his father-in-law called him "a loser."

Jim was an outgoing child, always seeking attention. He watched television endlessly, not for entertainment but to study and impersonate his favourite stars. Later, he perfected those impressions and used them in his professional comedy acts.

In junior high, Jim disrupted classes with zany comedy antics so often that his frustrated teacher allowed him 10 minutes at the end of each day to entertain his classmates. At the age of 10, Jim mailed his resume to the producers of *The Carol Burnett Show*. He also tried to publish a book of his poetry. Neither produced any results.

When Jim was in grade nine, the family suffered a major upset when Percy lost his job. The Carreys were forced to move to the industrial town of Scarborough on the outskirts of Toronto where each member of the family took menial jobs at the Titan Wheels Factory to make ends meet. Each day after school, young Jim worked eight-hour shifts scrubbing toilets and performing other exhausting duties. Naturally, his schooling suffered, and at age 16, he dropped out of high school altogether.

Desperately wanting to escape this bleak life, he set his sights on pursuing a career in show business. Early in his career, he wrote a $20 million cheque to himself that he kept in his wallet for years as a visualization of his future success. Jim worked on polishing and perfecting his stand-up act. Jim's father, like his mother, suffered from depression, but encouraged Jim and even helped write some of Jim's routines.

Jim's debut at the famed Yuk Yuk's was a disaster. Still, he was determined to make it, and worked out the kinks in his act at smaller Toronto clubs. He noticed that audiences enjoyed his impersonations, where he captured the voice and often also, eerily, the facial appearance of his subject, such as Henry Fonda in *On Golden Pond*.

In 1979, 17-year-old Jim travelled to Los Angeles. He landed a regular gig at The Comedy Store, where he often received standing ovations. One night comedian Rodney Dangerfield caught his act and asked Jim to come with him on tour as his support act. Jim was elated and looked upon this opportunity as his "big break."

Despite some ingenious improvised banter onstage between the veteran and the new kid, Jim's star failed to rise, and he watched with envy as other comedians of his generation, such as Arsenio Hall and Sam Kinison, saw their careers skyrocket.

Jim received an offer to appear on Johnny Carson's *Tonight Show* but was disappointed when he was not invited to sit beside Johnny after his act, the invitation being a sure sign that a comedian had "made it."

Jim was offered work, but mainly in forgettable low-budget Canadian productions. He appeared in *All in Good Taste* (1983), where he played a small role as a cameraman, and *Introducing…Janet*, playing a small part as comedian Tony Moroni (the film was later re-released as *Rubberface* to capitalize on Carrey's success). He appeared in *Club Med*, where he played the zany friend of comedian Alan Thicke.

Comparisons to Jerry Lewis already began to surface, and so it was fitting that he played a Lewis impersonator on *Buffalo Bill*, a short-lived comedy series that starred Dabney Coleman and Geena Davis. Unfortunately, Jim did not receive any onscreen credit for his bit.

Jim was fuelled with limitless energy and ambition and was discouraged at how slowly his career was progressing. When he auditioned for a part in the 1984 comedy *D.C. Cab*, he blew away producer Joel Schumacher but did not get the role because Schumacher believed Jim's manic personality would steal the picture away from its star, the volatile Mr. T. It was clear Jim needed a film of his own.

The opportunity to be the lead in a film arose when Jim was offered the role of Skip Tarketon, a young animator working on the Dippy Duck show on a new sitcom *The Duck Factory* (1984). But Jim never got to display his unique talents on the show because he played his character straight, and *The Duck Factory* failed after 13 episodes.

He was again down the cast list when he appeared in Richard Lester's surprisingly unfunny *Finders Keepers* (1984) about the hunt for treasure aboard a train. Future stars Louis Gossett Jr. and Beverly D'Angelo also had roles in the film.

Jim was awarded another leading role in the vampire "comedy" *Once Bitten* (1985), which starred gap-toothed former model Lauren Hutton. Hutton played The Countess, a vampire on the prowl who needs the blood of a virgin to retain her youth. Jim was Mark Kendall, whose main motivation in the movie was to "get it on" with Karen Kopins. The film tried to capture the humour of the earlier *Love at First Bite* (1979), but was a dismal failure, critically and commercially.

All of Jim's films thus far had performed miserably at the box office. Within a year, his money ran out. When he was doing well financially with the *Duck Factory* television series and film work, he had invited his parents to live with him at his house in L.A. Now he was forced to send them back to Toronto while he sought work.

Jim was down but not out. He realized that his career needed a new direction. He stopped doing impressions and returned to the zaniness of skit comedy. On the comedy circuit, he became fearless. During a memorable appearance on *The Arsenio Hall Show*, he played it so nervous in front of the audience that he pretended to wet himself onstage.

In 1986, Jim had an audition for *Saturday Night Live*, alongside Dana Carvey and Phil Hartman, but he did not show up for the audition. On his way to the NBC studios, he found himself in a large crowd watching a company employee threatening to commit suicide by throwing himself from the NBC sign. Jim realized he could not act funny after witnessing such a sight.

He continued to work in movies, appearing as Nicolas Cage's friend in *Peggy Sue Got Married* (1986) and then (billed as James Carrey) he played the drugged-out rock star Johnny Squares in Clint Eastwood's fifth Dirty Harry movie *The Dead Pool* (1988). Despite giving good performances, neither part enhanced his career.

In 1986, he experienced good fortune when he met waitress Melissa Womer at a comedy club. They married the following year and on September 6, 1987, had a daughter named Jane Erin.

In 1989 Jim did a small bit as comedian "James Carrey" in his friend Clint Eastwood's production *Pink Cadillac*. His next picture was the alien comedy *Earth Girls Are Easy* (1989). He was billed beneath real-life couple Geena Davis and Jeff Goldblum. Also in the cast was a young black comic named Damon Wayans. He and his brother Keenan Ivory were putting together an all-black comedy television series to be called *In Living Color*. They were looking to add a "token white" to the cast, and Damon enthusiastically suggested Jim, who hastened to come aboard. Jim (once again billed as James Carrey) fit the show like a glove, working as a writer on the series and creating outrageous characters, such as the notorious Fire Marshall Bill. Fire Marshall Bill was hugely popular with audiences, but aroused controversy when concerns were expressed over the "safety" advice Bill was giving children.

In Living Color became a hit and was Jim's greatest success yet. His popularity was definitely on the rise, and after that series was cancelled in 1991, Jim was given his own TV special, *Jim Carrey: The Un-Natural Act*. The series provided a springboard not only for Jim, but also for Chris Rock, Jamie Foxx, *Fly Girl* choreographer Rosie Perez and *Fly Girl* Jennifer Lopez.

During the run of *In Living Color*, Jim was presented with a quirky movie script thought to be perfect for him. At first Jim's hectic schedule prevented him from taking on the project. Finally in 1992, Jim accepted the title role of *Ace Ventura: Pet Detective*. By agreeing to do the movie, Jim subjected himself to a gruelling schedule. For four months, each day after rehearsals for *In Living Color*, he rushed to the film set and worked from midnight until 4:00 AM, perfecting one of the most off-the-wall characters ever seen on the screen.

Made for $12 million (of which Jim received $350,000), *Ace Ventura* (1994) earned $72 million. Jim was finally establishing himself as a box office draw.

After the two zany years on *In Living Color*, Jim chose a sombre subject for his next project. *Doing Time on Maple Drive* (1992) was a made-for-television movie that saw Jim as Tim Carter, the alcoholic son of a severely dysfunctional family. The role proved that Jim could act in dramas as effectively as comedies.

His next movie, *The Mask*, was again offbeat. He played mild-mannered bank clerk Stanley Ipkiss who discovers an ancient mask that transforms him into a gyrating, wisecracking superhero.

Man on the Moon (1999)

Co-starring Cameron Diaz, *The Mask* showcased Jim's most crazed, energetic performance to date, and earned him a Golden Globe nomination. The picture surpassed *Ace Ventura* in box office revenue. Jim continued his upward momentum.

Hoping to strike gold for a third time that year, Jim didn't stray from his proven formula and starred in the kooky comedy *Dumb and Dumber*, directed by Peter Farrelly. Jim was Eric Christmas while Jeff Daniels (an actor not known for comedies) played his dopier friend Harry Dunne. The film was an infantile road movie, but it scored with audiences.

During the making of *Dumb and Dumber*, Jim had an affair with his co-star Lauren Holly. The liaison cost him his marriage, and he and Melissa divorced in 1995, although he is still very close to his daughter. He and Lauren were married in September, 1996. Lauren continued with her career, appearing with Harrison Ford in *Sabrina* (1995) and Ray Liotta in *Turbulence* (1997). Work pressures soon caused a rift between the couple, and Jim and Lauren divorced in July 1997.

While Jim was not winning at romance, he was doing well professionally. Jim was asked to play The Riddler in *Batman Forever* (1995), which starred Val Kilmer as the Caped Crusader, Chris O'Donnell as Robin and Tommy Lee Jones as the sinister Two-Face. Jim pulled out all the stops in his acting, as did partner-in-crime Jones, leaving the Julliard-educated Kilmer with practically nothing to do. While probably the weakest in the

Batman series plotwise, the film exploded at the box office. Critics and audiences agreed that Jim's manic portrayal stole the show.

The success of *Ace Venture* naturally called for a sequel, and so that same year, Jim reprised the character in *Ace Ventura: When Nature Calls*. The film was as zany as the first and proved popular with audiences.

Jim's box office clout was phenomenal, which was why he was offered a $20 million payday to appear in his next feature *The Cable Guy* (1996). Jim took a risk with the role as a lonely cable repairman who insinuates himself into the life of a hapless customer played by Matthew Broderick. The risk didn't pay off; the picture was a commercial failure.

Rumours began circulating that Jim Carrey's meteoric rise had peaked and was beginning its descent. Many in the industry envied Jim and his $20 million salary. Many claimed that he'd achieved success too quickly and that he hadn't paid his dues. In fact, Jim had long since paid his dues, and he was a long way from being finished.

Liar, Liar (1997) offered Jim his best part up to that point. He played Fletcher Reede, an attorney who is also a compulsive liar. When circumstances suddenly prevent Reede from telling a single fib for 24 hours, he finds his life in a state of confusion. The situation starts a series of hilarious events in both Reede's personal and professional lives. The film, a huge success, put Jim back on track and earned him his second Golden Globe nomination.

He enjoyed equal success with *The Truman Show* (1998), where he played Truman Burbank, an insurance salesman living in a small seaside community who doesn't know that his whole life is a TV show. The film scored critically and commercially, and Jim's effective, subdued performance won him a Golden Globe Award. He was thought to be a strong contender for an Oscar nomination, but was overlooked.

Carrey's next film was also overlooked by people in the industry—the biography of eccentric comedian Andy Kaufmann titled *Man on the Moon* (1999). Kaufmann (1949–84) was known as much for his confrontations as his comedy on *SNL* and *Taxi*. Jim, who shared Andy's birthday (January 17), gave a stunning performance that won him a second Golden Globe. Many critics found fault with the film, but few criticized Jim's brilliant impersonation. People on the set who knew Kaufmann said it was almost as if the comic's personality possessed Jim during the making of the movie. Despite the praise, *Man on the Moon* was a commercial failure.

Once more, Jim needed another hit, and he found what he thought was a surefire winner in *Me, Myself and I* (2000), a typical Carrey concept. Jim plays a mild-mannered state trooper who develops an alter ego that allows him to unleash years of pent-up fury. Directed by the Farrelly brothers, the picture had the right elements going for it, including co-star Renée Zellweger, but did not score the big numbers expected for a Jim Carrey movie. A better result of the movie was that Jim and Zellweger hit it off during the filming.

Top decision-makers in Hollywood still saw potential in Jim. One of the biggest, director Ron Howard, envisioned Jim as the title character in his live-action version of that perennial Dr. Seuss favourite *How the Grinch Stole Christmas*. It was a demanding role, made worse by the heavy costuming and prosthetic makeup Jim was required to wear. According to press releases for the film, Jim received torture resistance training from a Navy SEAL to prepare for the long hours in makeup. One day, when Jim complained about how uncomfortable he was under the hot klieg lights, Ron Howard appeared on the set dressed in the exact same costume and directed the day's shoot in the Grinch body suit. Jim was impressed with Howard's consideration and finished the movie without complaint. While not critically regarded, *The Grinch Who Stole Christmas* (2000) was popular family fare, with the picture generating huge ticket sales.

Jim's personal life took another positive turn when he and Renée Zellweger were publicly announced as an item. Renée had scored her first big screen success opposite Tom Cruise in 1996's *Jerry Maguire* and looked to become a major star. They announced their engagement and made plans for their wedding. However, Jim and Renée's romantic pairing provided good copy for the paparazzi. The pressures placed on them by the press and Renée's extended stay in Britain while filming *Bridget Jones's Diary* (2001) soon ended their relationship. Jim said at the time, "I really want to love someone but just can't do it forever."

Fortunately, Jim had his work to console him, and in his next picture *The Majestic* (2001), he took on a role unlike any he had played before. He appeared as Peter Appleton, a blacklisted screen-writer who is called to testify before the House Un-American Activities Committee in 1951. After being involved in a car accident, Peter suffers amnesia and is taken to a small town where he is "recognized" as the missing soldier son of the owner of the local cinema. As had occurred in his past attempts at "drama," the public did not buy it. For all its noble intentions, *The Majestic* bombed…majestically.

A project with fascinating possibilities was Joel Schumacher's *Phone Booth* (2003), but Jim rejected it. It is interesting to speculate how the hyperactive Jim Carrey would have performed lengthy scenes where his character is confined inside a telephone booth.

Instead, Jim returned to comedy. He produced and starred in *Bruce Almighty*. In the film he played Bruce Nolan, a frustrated wannabe TV anchorman who blames God for his troubles and is surprised when the Almighty Himself (played by Morgan Freeman, in a brilliant and unexpected stroke of casting) grants him the power to see if he can do any better. *Bruce Almighty* caught on with audiences and was a commercial success. This was fortunate as Jim's salary had risen to $25 million per picture.

Jim is grateful for his success. Hollywood sources say he is a kind and generous man. Given his early years of struggle, he feels very fortunate for his success.

Eternal Sunshine of the Spotless Mind (2004) was a Jim Carrey showcase. It is not an exaggeration to say that Jim has never committed a finer or more complex performance to celluloid. The plot is convoluted and demands the viewer's patience, but the results are worth it.

Jim's schedule remains busy. Released in time for Christmas 2004 was the $140 million *Lemony Snicket's A Series of Unfortunate Events*, where Jim was cast as the rococo Count Olaf, a horrendous cad plotting the murder of the orphaned children of a dead distant relative. It is another performance where Jim pulls out all the stops and successfully walks the tightrope between obnoxiousness and comedy.

One of Jim's upcoming projects is the movie version of the '70s television hit *The Six Million Dollar Man* in which he'll play astronaut Steve Austin, the role made famous by Lee Majors.

Jim is also producing and starring in a remake of the 1977 George Segal/Jane Fonda crime romp *Fun With Dick and Jane*. The film details the plight of a middle-aged, middle-income couple who are suddenly and unexpectedly thrust into unemployment and decide to take economic matters into their own hands through a bank-robbery spree. Although the original version made no significant impact on audiences, Jim recognizes the comedic

The Truman Show (1998)

possibilities of the concept. He has decided to have the film take place in the new millennium.

There will also be a long-anticipated collaboration between Jim and Steven Spielberg in *The Secret Life of Walter Mitty*, a remake of the 1947 Danny Kaye classic.

Jim Carrey is an example of an actor who has reached the heights but still has a long way to go before he will feel he's reached creative fulfilment...if ever. He has excelled at both comedy and drama and effectively tackled the various nuances of each genre. Jim Carrey will be remembered by the parts he has chosen to play, including memorable excursions into the drama and has displayed a unique diversity of talent.

CHAPTER TWO

Mike Myers
(1963–)

MIKE MYERS IS PRESENTLY JIM CARREY'S CLOSEST COMPETITOR in the movie comedy sweepstakes. He has also built a career based on outrageous yet endearing characters that have definitely become part of our contemporary consciousness. Wayne Campbell of *Wayne's World* fame defined a generation of "mope-heads"—adolescent innocents devoid of any specific purpose in life other than to have a good time, but forever trying to grasp that elusive brass ring.

Austin Powers, likewise, is a character of dubious merit, a throwback to a bygone era—crude, garish, but possessed of qualities that give him a wide appeal to movie audiences.

Mike Myers has proved himself a creative genius. He honed his skills as one of the regulars on *Saturday Night Live* and expanded his comedic talents into a successful movie career. His versatility matches Jim's, with one exception. Although he still plays the absurd, there is less of the manic force so prevalent in Carrey's characterizations. Mike's playing is more subdued, yet no less effective. Mike Myers' characters are silly but possess the human foibles that viewers appreciate.

Michael Myers was born on May 25, 1963, in the Scarborough area of Toronto, which had been given the nickname "Scarberia" by snobby Torontonians. Mike's father Eric had been a cook in the British Army, while his mom Alice (also known as Bunny) had served in the RAF and was an aspiring actress who had attended London's Academy of Music and Dramatic Art. Mike's parents married in 1955 and immigrated to Canada the following year. Mike was the last of three sons born to the couple, following Paul (who later played in the band The Gravelberrys) and Peter. Mike's English (and Liverpool) background was pronounced. Until the age of six, he spoke with a Scouse (Liverpool) accent (that he shared with the Beatles dominating the airwaves at the time).

Canada provided a new start for the Myers clan. Bunny surrendered her acting ambitions to raise her three sons and take a job as a data processor. Eric sold the *Encyclopaedia Britannica*.

Mike's dad was a big fan of British comedy, and through him Mike was introduced to the British humour of Peter Sellers (Inspector Clouseau), Peter Cook and Dudley Moore. Eventually, this appreciation extended to the comedic insanity of *Monty Python's Flying Circus*. Mike was also fond of popular British TV drama shows of the time, including *The Avengers* and Roger Moore's *The Saint*.

Mike grew up in an environment conducive to his comic leanings. Dad Eric, for example, did not allow any friend of Mike's into the house if he felt the kid was not funny.

Mike was a cute child and began doing regular TV appearances at the age of eight. His commercial work included spots for Pepsi and Kit Kat bars. His most memorable television advertisement came when he was nine. He played the son of Gilda Radner (soon to achieve fame as one of the original Not Ready for Prime Time Players on Lorne Michaels' groundbreaking *Saturday Night Live*) in a BC Hydro ad. Mike enjoyed the experience so much that he vowed that someday he would act alongside Radner. He cried on the last day of shooting, for which his brothers nicknamed him "sucky-face," a nickname they still use today.

In later years, Mike became a leading member of *SNL*, but sadly that was the same year Gilda passed away after a long, courageous battle with breast cancer.

In the meantime, Mike was such a fan of *SNL* that when he was asked in grade eight to write a speech about the Canadian he most admired, he chose as his subject Lorne Michaels.

Mike attended the Stephen Leacock Collegiate Institute where he maintained a fair scholastic average. Where he excelled was in entertainment. He took dance lessons and began building a repertoire of characters, many of which he later used in his TV and film roles. Mike began his professional career the day he graduated from high school in 1982. He took his final exams at 9:00 AM and then rushed off to a noon audition with Toronto's famed Second City comedy troupe. By 3:00 PM, he was hired as a cast member.

Second City was formed in the early 1950s when a group of Chicago students, including Mike Nichols and Elaine May, teamed up with another bunch of theatrical wannabes (including Barbara Harris and Ed Asner) to create the Playwrights Theatre Club. In 1959, this group settled on its current name Second City that it retains to this day. By 1974, a branch had opened in Toronto that showcased the comedic talents of Dan Aykroyd, Bill Murray and John Candy, among others.

After Aykroyd and Murray moved on to roles on *Saturday Night Live*, the Toronto group created its own memorable television show. *SCTV* lasted seven seasons from 1976 to 1983, creating vignettes and unforgettable characters that are still popular today, such as the "hosers" Bob and Doug Mackenzie, now Canadian cultural icons.

Mike Myers was invited to join *SCTV* at the time the show began its downslide. Mike turned down the offer, realizing its popularity was sliding. Instead, he travelled to London to partner with a comic named Neil Mullarkey. Mike and Neil developed a comedy routine for their tour of UK. Overall they were successful, but British audiences did not appreciate some of their routine. An example was a children's program hosted by a fellow named Tommy Boyd. The show was called *The Wide Awake Club*. Mike was Boggles the Bounce, the underling of the main character Timmy Mallett, so named because he liked to hit small children over the head when they didn't answer his questions quickly enough.

Mike's career was progressing, but sadly his personal life was not faring as well. His father Eric was diagnosed with Alzheimer's disease and was deteriorating rapidly. He was not aware of the success his son was achieving.

Mike's accomplishments were indeed considerable. In 1988, Mike appeared at Second City's 15th anniversary party, where Martin Short noticed his talents. This led to an introduction to Lorne Michaels, who was quick to audition Mike for *Saturday Night Live.*

Mike was an immediate hit. For the next six years, he created an array of characters virtually unmatched in the program's 30-year run— Simon, the British lad who sat in his parents' bathtub and did drawings; Dieter, the host of the avant-garde German television show "Sprockets"; and "Coffee Talk" hostess Linda Richman, whom Mike admitted he based on his mother-in-law, to name a few. Wayne Campbell, the part he played to perfection opposite Dana Carvey's Garth, remains Mike's greatest contribution to the show. Wayne and Garth were presented as hosts of the cable offering "Wayne's World," telecast from Wayne's parents' basement and was about nothing at all. The characters provided audiences with a stream of verbiage not necessarily related to the English language.

Mike and his zany creations hit a nerve with the public, and he was nominated for an Emmy for "Best Performance in a Comedy or Variety Show."

However, he did not win the award, but he did win an Emmy for best writing in the same category.

Mike's success led to his being hired to both write and star in a feature based on his Wayne Campbell character, entitled *Wayne's World*. The picture featured a simplistic plot dealing with Wayne and Garth's public access TV show being acquired for mainstream broadcasting and the complications that ensue. While the film fell flat, individual scenes have become classic, such as the in-car "Bohemian Rhapsody" songfest and the Alice Cooper "We're not worthy!" segment played with...Alice Cooper. *Wayne's World* became a surprise hit, and the sixth highest grossing movie in the United States in 1992.

Once more, Mike's career success was counterbalanced by difficulties in his personal life. Dad Eric succumbed to his various ailments in 1991 shortly before the release of *Wayne's World*. His father's death was a devastating blow to Mike, and in memory of his dad Mike later named his production company Eric's Boy. Mike endured yet another tragedy when his brother was killed in a car crash.

He relied on his work to assuage his grief, and with the success of *Wayne's World*, there was no shortage of film offers. In 1993, Mike appeared in *So I Married an Axe Murderer*, playing the dual role of a mad Scottish father and his poet son. The son becomes involved with a sexy butcher whom he begins to suspect may be the villainess of the title.

While an adequate comedy, the picture was a major box office flop.

Wayne's World 2 was inevitable, given the video success of the first offering. Mike managed to line up a strong supporting cast, including Christopher Walken and Kim Basinger, but the film, released in 1993, offered nothing new. Domestic box office receipts were unimpressive.

This was a difficult time for Mike. He suffered from depression due to overwork and grief. A high point in his life was when he met Robin Ruzan at a bar following a hockey game. He married Robin on May 22, 1993, and decided to go into seclusion with his wife, his model soldiers, and his three dogs, which he named after hockey players.

During this seclusion, Myers created his greatest character. He recalled his youth with his dad and the great super-spy films they'd enjoyed, such as James Bond and Matt Helm, and he created *Austin Powers, International Man of Mystery.* Austin Powers was a creature of the 1960s, a secret agent who had been cryogenically frozen and thawed out into the present time to combat his old enemy, Dr. Evil. While Mike played the two main antagonists (for a $3 million paycheque), he rounded out his cast with Elizabeth Hurley, Michael York and an eye-patched Robert Wagner as Number Two.

Austin Powers seemed assured of a potent box office. However, the film became a financial success only when it was released to video. This success opened the door to a sequel.

Next, Mike played a rare straight role in *54*, as Steve Rubell, the cocaine-addicted boss of Studio 54. He followed that assignment with *Pete's Meteor* (1998), an Irish production where Mike played a secondary role that allowed him to use his talent at affecting accents. Although audiences did not love Pete's Meteor, it did attract critical attention in many circles, and Mike received positive notices for his playing.

The Thin Pink Line (1998) is another little-known Mike Myers movie, one that is hard to locate. This strange picture, in the form of a "mockumentary," presents quirky characters and boasts acting by *Friends* cast mates Jennifer Aniston and David Schwimmer.

Mystery, Alaska (1999) was next on Mike's agenda, and a picture he particularly wanted to do. Mike embraced the movie because of its central story of the title town's hockey team being given a once-in-a-lifetime chance to play against the New York Rangers. The film was shot in Mike's native Canada. Although of limited audience appeal, *Mystery, Alaska* features a sterling cast, including veteran Burt Reynolds holding his own against an up-and-coming Australian import named Russell Crowe. An extra reason for Mike to accept the role was that the film was to be directed by *Austin Powers* director Jay Roach.

One of Mike's greatest movie successes was in a part in which he was heard but not seen. *Shrek* (2001) was a computer-animated fable that told the story of an antisocial troll (Mike inherited the part after the unexpected death of Chris Farley) who, with a talkative donkey (voice of Eddie Murphy), goes on a quest to save the beautiful Princess Fiona (Cameron Diaz). To everyone's surprise, the film became a hit, earning almost $500 million worldwide.

Just as Mike's professional career was running at a high speed, he ran into difficulty with Universal with whom he had inked a lucrative deal following the success of *Wayne's World*. Mike had agreed to make a movie using his script called *Sprockets*, which was based on his Dieter character, but unsatisfied with the final screenplay, he refused to appear in the picture. He was quoted as saying that he'd rather reject a $20 million payday than "cheat the moviegoers with an unacceptable script." As a result, he faced a multi–million-dollar lawsuit against him both by Universal and Imagine Entertainment, the studio headed by Ron Howard and Brian Grazer.

Mike fought back and hit the studio with his own $20 million lawsuit, claiming that Universal had violated his right to privacy by hiring a writserver to stalk him and his wife "in a threatening manner." These difficulties were resolved through the efforts of Steven Spielberg and Jeffrey Katzenberg of DreamWorks, who arranged a deal for Mike to star in another Universal/Imagine collaboration, based on the famous Dr. Seuss story *The Cat in the Hat*.

Even though life once again seemed rosy for Mike, another dark cloud loomed on the horizon.

After filming the *Austin Powers* sequel *Austin Powers: The Spy Who Shagged Me* in 1999 (in which he assumed a third role, the disgusting Fat Bastard), MGM, who held the rights to the James Bond films, accused him of capitalizing on the James Bond license without permission. While no legal proceedings resulted on that picture, the same charges were levelled with a vengeance against the third movie in the *Austin Powers* franchise, *Austin Powers in Goldmember* (2002). The connection between this title and the 1964 hit *Goldfinger* was too close to be ignored. The problems were resolved, when MGM dropped its lawsuit with the proviso that the studio must approve all future Austin Powers titles. This proved to be a small concession as *Austin Powers in Goldmember* was one of the top moneymaking hits of the year, earning $310 million worldwide. The picture made history as the first sequel to earn a higher domestic gross than its predecessors.

The *Austin Powers* pictures also garnered a large number of awards, including several People's Choice Awards, Grammy Awards and Blockbuster Entertainment Awards. Mike was also presented with the American Comedy Award for Funniest Actor in a Movie. Naturally, there was talk of expanding upon the *Austin Powers* phenomenon, suggesting titles that included *Live and Let Shag, You Only Shag Twice* and *License to Shag*.

Instead, Mike went to work on *A View from the Top* (2003), where he appeared in a smallish role as a cross-eyed comic whose performance seems out of sync with the rest of the story. The problem might have been that the shooting of the picture was delayed following the 9/11 attacks, and one of Mike's best scenes showing him instructing his students how to behave during a terrorist siege was cut from the final print. *A View from the Top* opened in theatres two years after its completion…and promptly flopped at the box office.

Mike's next movie also flopped. *Nobody Knows Anything* is a dark comedy about two average men who decide to rob a grocery store. Mike's role as "Eye" Witness is brief and forgotten as quickly as the film itself.

Mike knew that he was taking risks with his career. But, undaunted, he ventured forward into new directions. His success as Austin Powers made him a leading candidate to play the role of the clumsy Inspector Clouseau in a proposed remake of *The Pink Panther*, but Mike was not interested in recreating a role that the late Peter Sellers had played to such perfection.

Mike wanted to create his own character, so accepted the lead role in *The Cat in the Hat.* Following the phenomenal 2000 Christmas success of *How the Grinch Stole Christmas,* Imagine Entertainment acquired the rights to what many consider Dr. Seuss's most endearing character. Unfortunately, *The Cat in the Hat* proved an instant critical misfire, due mainly to excessive silliness and adult themes not in line with the original Dr. Seuss stories. An ingenious marketing campaign managed to earn the movie a fair return.

Mike could now afford to step into a previous comic incarnation and reprise the role of Shrek in *Shrek 2* (2004). Although the sequel offered audiences nothing new, it was redeemed by the endearing characters from the original. *Shrek 2* proved to be another box office bonanza, bringing in an astounding $437 million domestically. Naturally, such success has led to the announcement of another *Shrek* sequel, tentatively scheduled for release in 2006.

Mike Myers has enjoyed a movie career that has barely spanned a decade. During this brief time, he has created an array of film characters who have become audience favourites, most prominently Wayne Campbell, Austin Powers, Dr. Evil (his personal favourite), Fat Bastard (his least favourite) and the comedic troll Shrek.

Mike has a difficult time defining his incredible success. "I'm basically a sexless geek. Look at me. I have pasty, white skin, I have acne scars and I'm five-foot-nothing [1.5 metres]. Does that sound like a real sexual dynamo to you?"

While Mike considers himself a British citizen, Canada is his birthplace and embraces him as one of its own. In 2003, he was awarded a star on the Canadian Walk of Fame in Toronto. Another tribute to his talents and contribution to the arts came when a street in Scarborough was named Mike Myers Drive.

Mike has a comical approach to Canada: "Canada is the essence of not being. Not English, not American. It is the mathematics of not being.

And a subtle flavour—we're more like celery as a flavour."

Mike remains a private man, devoted to wife Robin. He finds relaxation in collecting, making and painting model soldiers.

He is very proud of a letter he received from George Harrison where the ex-Beatle complimented Mike for his work in *Goldmember*. Mike framed the letter and looks at it every day, saying that receiving that letter is the most incredible thing that has ever happened to him.

Mike has incredible things on his professional horizon, such as *Shrek 3*, which is scheduled for 2006. Although there hasn't been a decision regarding a fourth Austin Powers movie, it is expected that audiences will be treated to further exploits of that 1960s furry-chested anachronism whose slang and stylings have become part of the contemporary consciousness.

CHAPTER THREE

Kim Cattrall
(1956–)

KIM CATTRALL HAS ENJOYED MANY YEARS AS AN ONSCREEN actress, appearing in a variety of television and motion picture roles. But she has achieved her greatest success on HBO's long-running *Sex and the City* (1998–2004), in which she co-starred with Sarah Jessica Parker (Carrie Bradshaw), Kristin Davis (Charlotte York) and Cynthia Nixon (Miranda Hobbes).

Kim played Samantha Jones, the sexually promiscuous public relations executive whose prowess in the bedroom often exceeded her skill in the boardroom. Kim created a memorable character and earned a Golden Globe nomination and an Emmy for her work. Despite her success with the role, she remains a versatile actress, adept at playing comedy and drama, and, while many of the movies in which she has appeared are not memorable, she has turned in many fine performances.

She was born Clare Woodgate in Liverpool, England, on August 21, 1956. She moved to Vancouver, BC, with her parents Dennis and Shane when she was three years old. She discovered a love of performing at an early age, and at 11, she returned

Sex and the City

to England to study at the London Academy of Music and Dramatic Arts. She returned to Canada following graduation and attended The Banff School of Fine Arts. At age 16, she won a scholarship to the American Academy of Dramatic Arts in New York.

After Kim's graduation from AADA, famed director Otto Preminger signed her to a five-year contract, and in 1975, 19-year-old Kim made her movie debut in Preminger's *Rosebud*. Kim worked with a strong cast, headed by Peter O'Toole and Richard Attenborough; but the film, one of the last the director made, was a critical and financial disaster.

Preminger sold Kim's contract to Universal, where the actress became part of the studio's contract player system. This system, by which young talent are groomed for stardom by participating in various lessons, such as speech, drama and dance while doing small parts in film and television, was popular in the 1950s, with some of the more notable participants being Rock Hudson and Tony Curtis.

During this period, Kim showed up in guest spots on such popular '70s TV programs as *Quincy*, *Starsky and Hutch*, *The Incredible Hulk* and *Charlie's Angels*. She also acted in a number of made-for-TV movies, including *Good against Evil* (1977) and a *Columbo* episode—*How to Dial a Murder*. Two of her more high-profile roles came in *The Gossip Columnist* (1979) and the soap opera mini-series *Scruples* (1979), where she played the small role of Melanie Adams.

Kim had no shortage of TV work, but she was eager to return to motion pictures. In 1980, she was awarded a somewhat larger role opposite Jack Lemmon in the Canadian feature *Tribute*. In this maudlin film, directed by Bob Clark, a Broadway press agent (Lemmon, who created the role on stage) learns he is dying, and tries to rebuild a relationship with his estranged son (Robby Benson). *Tribute* received mixed notices, but Kim was given good reviews.

Kim scored with her next project, *Ticket to Heaven* (1981), another Canadian production that dealt with a young man seduced into a "Moonie"-like cult. For her role as Ruthie, Kim was nominated for a Genie.

After two heavy, dramatic films, Kim branched out into comedy by playing Honeywell in the sophomoric but highly successful *Porky's* (1982). The film, directed by Bob Clark, grossed well at the box offices. Unfortunately, its success paved the way for two brain-numbing sequels.

Kim continued her run of zany films when she signed on to play Cadet Karen Thompson in *Police Academy* (1984), another box office winner of low critical merit (which also spawned a succession of ridiculous sequels).

Returning to serious film work, she appeared in the suspenseful TV movie *Sins of the Past*, where she plays one of a group of call girls who change their identities and go their separate way after a colleague is murdered. When they reunite 15 years later, they find that each has become successful at a new occupation, and the killer reappears. Kim played Paula Bennett, who became a doctor.

Following *Sins of the Past*, Kim appeared in an eclectic collection of roles. She co-starred opposite Timothy Hutton in the comedy *Turk 182* (1985), then she was seen in the quirky Canadian crime comedy *Hold Up*, starring one-time French superstar Jean-Paul Belmondo, and in the science fiction clunker *City Limits*. She had a role in John Carpenter's mixture of all genres, *Big Trouble in Little China* (1986). While this film gave Kim her best movie part to date, it was a critical and financial dud.

Kim's next film, *Mannequin* (1987), was another bomb. In the picture she played Ema Hesire, an ancient Egyptian spirit who possesses a department store mannequin. Its reasonable box office receipts resulted in an even worse sequel four years later.

In *Midnight Crossing*, Kim played opposite Faye Dunaway and former *Hill Street Blues* star Daniel J. Travanti. Alexa Schubb (Kim) is one of a group of adventurers who sneak into Cuba trying to recover $1 million in cash hidden when Fidel Castro took over in 1959. Leonard Maltin's *Movie Guide* regarded the film as "hokey, boring, [and] needlessly violent." While Kim's movies were generally forgettable, she often received kind words from critics, with one writer saying that she had an effervescent presence.

Kim returned to Canada to make a couple of features, the crime-romance *Palais Royale* (*Smoke Screen*) and *La Famiglia Buonanotte* (*Brown Bread*

Sandwiches)(1989), a touching film about immigrant Italian life in 1950s Canada.

That same year she played Justine de Winter in the British-French-Spanish co-production *The Return of the Musketeers*. Directed by Richard Lester, the film was the third in the Musketeers series, which had begun with Lester's *The Three Musketeers* in 1974 and was followed by *The Four Musketeers* in 1975. Many members of the original cast returned for this latest instalment, including Michael York, Oliver Reed, Christopher Lee and Richard Chamberlain. C. Thomas Howell and Kim were the new faces. Unfortunately, this sequel did not have the lustre of the original and was not as well received.

After the dreadful *Honeymoon Academy* (1990), Cattrall appeared in a film that seemed to have all the right ingredients for a blockbuster. *The Bonfire of the Vanities*, based on the best-selling novel by Tom Wolfe, was directed by Brian De Palma, and boasts superstars Tom Hanks, Bruce Willis and Melanie Griffith. But something happened in the translation. The final product contained only the merest suggestion of Wolfe's story. Critics trashed the movie, and the public stayed away. The picture didn't even gross the salaries of its lead players.

Finally Kim enjoyed her biggest commercial success since *Police Academy* when she won the role of Lieutenant Valeris in *Star Trek VI: The Undiscovered Country* (1990). Besides William Shatner, the movie starred fellow Canadian Christopher Plummer as General Chang, a treacherous Klingon who attempts to sabotage a treaty between the

Big Trouble in Little China (1986)

Federation and the Klingon Empire. The picture earned well at the box office, with many fans considering *Star Trek VI* the best in the series. Kim enjoyed a good role in an audience-proof movie. Unfortunately, it was one of her last box office successes.

Although Kim preferred film to television, she continued to work in both mediums and seemed to do better on TV. She had roles in such washouts as the futuristic *Split Second* (1992), and the Canadian-made crime thriller *Breaking Point* (1993). It is interesting to note that her role of Jamie in *Live Nude Girls* bears a strong resemblance to Samantha on *Sex and the City*. In *Crossroads* (2002), she played opposite pop singer Britney Spears who had her movie debut in that film.

Kim also found artistic satisfaction on the stage. She made her debut on Broadway opposite the distinguished Ian McKellen in the National Theater's production of Anton Chekhov's *Wild Honey*. She also starred in Moliere's *The Misanthrope* and in Strindberg's *Miss Julie* and received acclaim for her work in Arthur Miller's *A View from the Bridge*.

Most audiences recognize Kim Cattrall best for her six seasons on *Sex and the City*. Based on the writings of *New York Observer* columnist Candace Bushnell, the saucy show dealt with four beautiful New Yorkers who talk about their sex lives while coping with being women in the '90s. The series became a surprise hit, starting trends and, more importantly, establishing each of its lead actors as stars. At the 2000 MTV movie awards,

Kim and her co-stars appeared in a hilarious spoof of the series titled *Sex and the Matrix*. Kim has certainly benefited from the show, and as the series was winding down in 2003, it was announced that her character would star in her own spin-off series.

Until the spin-off series materializes (if it does), Kim remains busy, and her film choices remain eccentric, appearing in serious films like *15 Minutes* (2001), where she worked with Robert De Niro and Edward Burns. Kim has also appeared in nonsense like *Modern Vampires* (1998) and *Baby Geniuses* (1999). She remains a regular fixture in TV movies, where she gave good performances in Robin Cook's *Invasion* (1998) and Peter Benchley's *Creature* (1998).

There is more to Kim Cattrall than her movie and television roles suggest. In 2001 she was voted one of *People Magazine*'s "25 Most Intriguing People of 2001." That year, fans got the chance to learn something about her when she was profiled on *Intimate Portrait: Kim Cattrall*. The TV program revealed that Kim is an avid skier, enjoys writing short stories and is an advocate for senior citizens' rights. Kim has been romantically involved with a number of high-profile men, including Pierre Trudeau and actor Daniel Benzali. Married twice previously, she married Mark Levinson on September 4, 1998. They make their home in New York.

Kim's next film is titled *Ice Princess* and is currently in post-production, scheduled for a 2005 release.

Dan Aykroyd
(1952–)

Dᴀɴ Aʏᴋʀᴏʏᴅ ʜᴀs ᴘʀᴏᴠᴇɴ ʜɪᴍsᴇʟғ ᴀ ᴛʀᴜᴇ ɢᴇɴɪᴜs ᴏғ ʙᴏᴛʜ cinematic comedy and drama. He first made an impact as one of the innovative talents on Lorne Michaels' groundbreaking TV series *Saturday Night Live*. From there he branched out into comedic film roles and then into more serious parts. In the process, he earned himself a reputation as a versatile actor.

With cohort John Belushi, Dan created characters unparalleled in television history, specifically Elwood Blues in "The Blues Brothers" and Beldar Conehead in "The Coneheads" skits.

Dan Aykroyd can best be described as a manic talent, filled with a perverse creativity that has seen him advance from humble beginnings with Toronto's Second City comedy club through national television exposure into one of the premiere talents in motion pictures.

Daniel Edward Aykroyd was born in Ottawa on July 1, 1952. Dan's father, Samuel Cuthbert Peter Hugh Aykroyd, could trace his British ancestry back to a 14th-century police constable. Samuel

worked as a civil engineer and then became a private consultant before assuming the rank of Canada's Deputy Minister of Transportation. Dan's mother Lorraine was of French-Canadian descent and was employed as an executive secretary with the Canadian government.

As a child, Dan was diagnosed with Tourette's Syndrome and Asperger Syndrome, although the symptoms mostly subsided by the time he was 14. Dan was an active child whose mischievous behaviour often brought him strappings, and his delinquency eventually led to his arrest for drunkenness in New York.

Fortunately, Dan channelled some of his aggressiveness into more creative pursuits, and at the age of 12 he began playing the drums and participating in improvisational theatre. While attending St. Pius X Preparatory Seminary, Dan enjoyed mimicking the nuns and priests of the school, spending more time perfecting his impersonations than on his studies. He was eventually expelled from the school for committing acts of minor delinquency. Dan graduated from a co-ed Catholic school before enrolling at Carleton University in Ottawa. His course load included psychology, political science and criminal sociology.

He was a rebellious student. "I was a loud-mouthed, flagrant fool," he admitted in an interview. However, during his college years, Dan did develop a work ethic. He worked at a variety of menial jobs, prompting him to state in a 1983 interview with *US* magazine: "To this day I still have that blue-collar mentality."

Dan continued to enjoy theatre and was active in Carleton's Sock and Buskin Drama Guild. Another of his pleasures was playing the harmonica (a talent he developed during a summer in the Northwest Territories).

Dan never completed his graduate studies at Carleton, leaving college after four years. He worked as a mail sorter for Canada Post, where he made the acquaintance of another young acting hopeful named John Candy. Dan then took a job as a fast-talking television pitchman that paid him $35 a week. He also began more substantial creative endeavours by producing, co-writing and acting in a series of 15-minute comedy shorts released under the title of *A Change for a Quarter*, funded by a private cable television company. He also was a writer and a featured player in a CBC children's show called *Coming Up Rosie*. As if his creative work wasn't keeping him busy, Dan and a couple of friends opened an after-hours bistro called The Club 505.

By 1972, Dan had enough of a reputation to be invited to join the newly formed Toronto offshoot of the Chicago-based improvisational group, Second City. In 1974, Dan joined the Chicago cast, where his talent for impersonations caught the eye of Lorne Michaels. Michaels hired Dan to be one of the lead performers for his new NBC series *Saturday Night Live* at a salary of $750 per week. The program was broadcast live from New York City three times a month and presented 90 minutes of comedy skits and featured a weekly musical guest. Dan joined an impressive ensemble, most of whom later parlayed their talents into successful motion picture careers—Chevy Chase, Bill Murray, Gilda Radner, Garrett Morris, Laraine Newman and his best pal John Belushi.

Dan became the "chameleon" of the cast, perfecting impersonations of Richard Nixon, Robert Stack, Jimmy Carter, Tom Snyder and Julia Child. He proved adept at creating offbeat characters, including E. Buzz Miller, the sleazy host of a public access cable TV show, and Leonard Pinth-Garnell, renowned for his hosting chores on "Bad Theatre." Another of Dan's memorable creations was the patriarch of the Conehead brood, a family of extra-terrestrials with enlarged craniums who were trying to adapt to life on Earth.

Dan reached his peak playing Elwood Blues opposite John Belushi's Jake in "The Blues Brothers" segments. Dan and John became close both professionally and personally. Dan described his first meeting with John Belushi in 1973: "As soon as we met, there was an instant rapport. It was like Stanley meeting Livingstone." There hadn't been such an effective pairing between physically mismatched comics since Abbott and Costello.

At the time, Dan was doing both his *SNL* chores and his first movie role in *Love at First Sight* (1974), which was filmed in Toronto. The 85-minute "comedy" told the story of a blind young man

(Aykroyd) in love with a young woman. Most reviewers found the film "excruciating."

Dan and Belushi began their teamwork during the second season of *Saturday Night Live*. They combined their creative talents to write comedic sketches, a labour-intensive task of which Dan later said, "Without exaggeration, we required a 72-hour week." It was a crazy, surreal existence. Dan and Belushi often shared quarters for days on end at NBC's Rockefeller Center studios where they shared an office, slept in bunk beds and subsisted on pizza, all the while trying to come up with new gags and sketches for the show.

This did not prove the ideal environment. As Lorne Michaels later reported: "John was never patient as a writer; Danny was meticulous. John didn't have the attention span for writing a sketch; whereas Danny would stay there until he died for it." But rather than creating a rift between the two, this close-quarter relationship strengthened the friendship between Dan and Belushi and was the spawning ground for new characters.

The two created The Blues Brothers. It was Dan, a long time fan of the blues, who introduced Belushi to his personal music preference and then put him in a dark suit, fedora and sunglasses. The Blues Brothers act was never intended to be anything more than a warm-up gig for *SNL*. However, the pair became an immediate hit with audiences and was even booked to appear as the opening act for Steve Martin during his performance at the Universal Amphitheater in Los Angeles.

Aykroyd and Belushi next went to a recording label and released their first album *Briefcase Full of Blues* in 1978, which sold two million copies and earned them a Grammy nomination. The Blues Brothers capitalized on their success by embarking on a 10-city tour during which they produced the live album *Made in America*, followed by their 1980 25-city tour which resulted in the duo's third and final album *Best of The Blues Brothers*.

It was while appearing as an opening act for Steve Martin that Dan and John learned that they had been chosen for roles in Steven Spielberg's upcoming mega-dollar production, *1941*. It was an exciting proposition for both performers, though not their first experience on celluloid. John Belushi had scored a hit in *National Lampoon's Animal House*, a surprising sleeper directed by John Landis. Dan's introduction to movies *Love at First Sight* had come and gone with hardly a notice. Dan probably wished that his contribution to the vehicle had been ignored. The July 20, 1977 issue of *Variety* reported: "Only the most juvenile mind would find this attempt at comedy even remotely interesting....It is hamstrung by heavy-handed acting by Dan Aykroyd." This review stood in strong contrast to the flowering compliments Belushi received for his work in *Animal House*.

But in *1941* (released in 1979), Dan held his own against Belushi. He played a gung ho tank sergeant alongside Belushi's National Guard pilot. Despite its reported $40 million cost, the picture dive-bombed at the box office and provided Spielberg with his first flop after his successes with *Jaws* (1975) and *Close Encounters of the Third Kind* (1977).

Dan married Maureen Lewis about this time and the couple had three sons—Mark, Lloyd and Oscar. They later divorced.

Both Aykroyd and Belushi decided to take advantage of their burgeoning movie careers and departed *SNL* in 1979 prior to the show's fourth season. Dan had already recorded two more comedy videos, *The Best of Dan Aykroyd*, a compilation of 15 *SNL* sketches in which he appeared, and a follow-up titled *One More Saturday Night*. Dan had a lot of creative input during his four years on *SNL*, and in 1977 he was awarded with an Emmy for his writing contributions to the show.

A year after the *1941* bomb, Dan and Belushi fared better with *The Blues Brothers* (1980). The feature film, co-written by Dan and director John Landis, didn't set box offices ablaze, but did establish Dan Aykroyd as a motion picture star. Admittedly, the overlong (exceeding two hours) movie didn't have much of a plot: Deadpan entertainers Elwood and Jake Blues try to raise funds in order to save the orphanage they were raised in by reuniting their blues band and nearly destroy the city of Chicago in the process.

Despite Dan's comedic talents, his next film cast him in an obnoxious role opposite John Belushi. The part evidently was meant to be funny, but what emerged onscreen did not have subtlety or humour. *Neighbors* (1981) tried to be a perverse Jack Lemmon/Walter Matthau-type comedy but turned out to be what *New York Daily News* film columnist Rex Reed described as "a slimy, vulgar piece of trash." Reed was just one of many U.S. critics who trashed the movie. The negative reviews were unfortunate as the actors took chances with this film. Belushi took a change-of-pace role as the sedate character in the picture against the obnoxious Dan role, rather than the other way around as was usually the case.

Sadly, the teaming of the two comics was halted forever when John Belushi died of a drug overdose on March 5, 1982. Dan was devastated by his friend's death. In an interview with Gene Siskel of the *Chicago Tribune*, he said: "More than missing the work we might have done together, I miss him. He was a friend I could call at any time of the day or night. He was always happy to see me, and I was always happy to see him. There was very little friction between us. I can't think of any argument that ever lasted for more than 24 hours. It was one of the great friendships of the decade, if not the century." Dan, clad in a leather jacket and mounted on his motorcycle, led Belushi's funeral procession.

After Belushi's death, Dan kept busy. One of his projects was performing as an on-camera host (along with John Candy, Cheech and Chong and Gilda Radner) for *It Came from Hollywood* (1982), a compilation of the worst in Hollywood. The film proved a total box office flop. He then played the role of a meek college professor who leads the life of a Chicago gangster in *Doctor Detroit* (1983). This was another film that failed to thrill critics and audiences.

However, the picture was not a total disaster for Dan. During the shoot, he established a close relationship with co-star Donna Dixon (best known for her role as the blonde bombshell on TV's *Bosom Buddies,* which co-starred Tom Hanks in his first prominent role). The two married on April 29, 1983. This was Dan's second marriage and stands as one of the happier Hollywood unions.

Dan's next cinematic venture proved to be a huge hit. In *Trading Places,* Dan co-starred with another *SNL* alumnus, Eddie Murphy, now riding the crest of his own popularity following the success of *48 Hours* (1982). Both the inspired casting (which included supporting parts played by veterans Ralph Bellamy and Don Ameche) and the picture's concept depicting a wealthy man (Aykroyd) switching places with a penniless street hustler (Murphy) scored with critics as well as with the movie-going public. Dan received the best reviews he had ever received. Rex Reed in his *New York Post* review of the movie, enthused: "I expected another trashy Dan Aykroyd farce. Instead I got a film with real wit and imagination, populated by interesting and amusing characters, and featuring the most consistently sustained piece of acting Aykroyd has yet managed in a feature film. He is splendid."

Dan's next films provided him with cameo roles, in the comical but frightening prologue to *Twilight Zone: The Movie* and *Indiana Jones and the Temple of Doom* (1984), the sequel to Steven Spielberg's 1981 mega-hit *Raiders of the Lost Ark.*

In 1984, Dan also finished co-writing a film based on one of his passions, the paranormal, and the result was the smash hit *Ghostbusters*. Originally intended as a co-starring vehicle for Dan and John Belushi, the latter's untimely death led to the casting of Bill Murray. Aykroyd, co-scripter Harold Ramis and Murray played a ghost-hunting trio. *Ghostbusters* enjoyed a June release and virtually devoured all competition during its lengthy summer run. The movie became the highest-grossing comedy of all time, a record it enjoyed until the 1990 release of *Home Alone*.

Dan's career certainly peaked with *Ghostbusters*. His next films saw him in supporting roles, including *Nothing Lasts Forever* and *Into the Night*. His next major movie role was in *Spies Like Us* (1985), which he again co-wrote and in which he starred opposite another *SNL* cohort, Chevy Chase. Apparently, Dan hoped to capture the box office potential of a spy spoof as he had done successfully with the supernatural, but sadly *Spies Like Us* fell short of his expectations both critically and financially.

Dan next helped write a script parodying the detective genre, choosing as his project a remake of television's best-known police procedural series *Dragnet* (1987). Dan played the part of Joe Friday, the nephew of the original cop, a role made famous by Jack Webb, and delivered a letter-perfect deadpan impersonation of Webb, even sporting Webb's trademark crewcut. Once again, Dan received excellent notices. Gene Siskel of the *Chicago Times* wrote: "With his tongue planted firmly in his cheek, Dan Aykroyd gives the performance of his career."

Dan was singled out for critical praise, but the film itself, co-starring Tom Hanks, was not as positively regarded. Representative of the reviews was one written by Mike McGrady of *New York Newsday* who called *Dragnet* a "one-joke comedy." The film also failed to have significant pull at the box office.

Dan appeared in four films in 1988, including *The Couch Trip*, where he played John Burns, an escaped mental patient who masquerades as a Beverly Hills psychiatrist and becomes a popular radio call-in sex therapist. While the film wasn't a success, Dan's performance again garnered favourable critical reaction. Chris Chase of the *New York Daily News* reported: "The plot is sheer bedlam. Even a five-year-old couldn't suspend disbelief. But it brings back the great Dan Aykroyd of *Saturday Night Live*, as free and loony as they come."

Dan's next three films hardly did justice to his comedic talents. He played opposite his Canadian buddy and former Second City cohort John Candy in *The Great Outdoors*, which despite their combined efforts and a script written by John Hughes, produced only scattershot laughs and a poor ticket sales.

Caddyshack II fared no better, and sadly Dan was singled out for terrible reviews. Rita Kempley of the *Washington Post* was particularly critical, writing, "Aykroyd has never been so awful."

My Stepmother is an Alien was Dan's third movie misfire that year, despite the presence of the glamorous Kim Basinger as the title character. Once again, Dan received miserable notices, with Kathleen Carroll of the New York *Daily News* writing "[Aykroyd's] no more fun to watch than your average couch potato."

Dan was desperate for a hit, and he chose as his next film a sequel to his biggest critical and commercial success thus far. For *Ghostbusters II* (1989), Dan again co-wrote the script with Harold Ramis and recruited Bill Murray to reprise his role as Dr. Peter Venkman. While not as successful as the first film, *Ghostbusters II* was the fifth highest-grossing movie of the year.

At this point, Dan had achieved a significant reputation as a comedian, but had not been given the opportunity to display his dramatic abilities. That changed with his role in *Driving Miss Daisy* (1989), where he played Boolie Werthan, the son of a well-to-do Southern widow (Jessica Tandy) who over a 25-year period develops a friendship with her black chauffeur (Morgan Freeman).

This role was important to Dan personally as much as it was professionally. He understood the liberal leanings of his character, explaining: "I'm not Jewish. But I am half French-Canadian. I went to an English school, so I was always getting beat up. I understand racial hatred and mistrust."

Dan's performance (marred as it was by obvious old-age makeup) garnered him a Best Supporting Oscar nomination, which Chevy Chase in an

Academy Award presentation that evening acknowledged with affection and respect. While an audience favourite, Dan lost the award to Denzel Washington for his sympathetic role in the U.S. Civil War drama *Glory*. *Driving Miss Daisy* won four other Oscars that night including Best Picture and provided Dan with an opening to a career as a dramatic actor.

Unfortunately, Dan did not immediately capitalize on the opportunity, choosing instead to play opposite Gene Hackman in one of that actor's rare excursions into farce—*Loose Cannons* (1990). This was followed by Dan's debut as a director in a film he wrote entitled *Nothing But Trouble*. The picture made low ticket sales and received no positive reviews.

In 1991, Dan gave a wonderfully understated performance in *My Girl*, where he played widowed undertaker Harry Sultenfuss, struggling to raise a precocious, hypochondriac 11-year-old daughter (Anna Chlumsky) while dealing with the affections of his beautician assistant (Jamie Lee Curtis). Co-starring Macauley Culkin in one of his last "cute" roles, *My Girl* did respectable business at the box office. Dan created a role completely different from his established character, and Janet Maslin of the *New York Times* described Dan Aykroyd, with his "rotund and rather hangdog" appearance, as a "very unlikely romantic lead." Even though the press panned his role, Jamie Lee Curtis, who acted with him in two movies, called him the best screen kisser who ever played a scene with her.

Now receiving more recognition for his dramatic talents, Dan was chosen by distinguished actor-turned-director Sir Richard Attenborough to portray fellow Canadian, silent movie pioneer Mack Sennett in Sir Richard's biopic of Charlie in *Chaplin* (1992). The picture was an ambitious depiction of the great Chaplin's public and private life, with a star-making performance by Oscar-nominated Robert Downey Jr., but the film, for all its intentions, failed to catch on with audiences.

Dan once more tried to capitalize on a successful formula by co-writing the movie version of *Coneheads* (1993). Although the 88-minute feature was an expanded rehash of old *SNL* sketches, it received favourable reviews, but *Coneheads* crashed with moviegoers.

Even with a career that some critics said was floundering, Dan was active in his profession. He didn't insist on star billing and so stayed in demand, even if that meant taking on small parts or even cameo roles in such films as *My Girl 2* (1994). In 1995, three films were released in which he had acted—Rob Reiner's *North, Exit to Eden* and *Tommy Boy*, where Dan's acting supported that of *SNL* stars Chris Farley and David Spade.

Returning to the small screen, Dan developed the CBC mini-series *The Arrow*, which was shot in Winnipeg in 1997. In the film he played Crawford Gordon, general manager of A.V. Roe Canada Ltd., the company that created the ill-fated aircraft. His straight-laced character was in contrast to the real Dan Aykroyd, a leather-jacketed misfit often spotted

roaring around the city on a motorcycle and fre-
quenting late-night blues bars.

Dan continued on television, playing Reverend
Mike Weber on the ABC sitcom *Soul Man*. Despite
favourable critical response, the network cancelled
the show after only one season.

Dan may have been disappointed by the failure of
this series, but he was pleased in 1997 to be
awarded with a Doctorate in Literature (*honoris
causa*) from Carleton University in recognition of his
numerous film and television writing credits. And
one of Dan's prouder moments was in 1999, when
he was named a member of The Order of Canada,
an honour bestowed upon prominent Canadians for
extraordinary merit and achievement.

Dan Aykroyd never became a leading man—his
talent for eccentric roles and comedy denied him
that opportunity, but he excels as a character actor.
He continues in that role today, enhancing such
pictures as *The Curse of the Jade Scorpion* and the
recent *Christmas with the Kranks* (2004) merely with
his screen presence.

Back on the small screen, Dan's interest in the
supernatural has him taking on the role of host
and co-producer of the television series *PSI: Chron-
icles of the Paranormal*. In this series he works with
his brother Peter, a psychic researcher who has
been hired as a consultant for the show.

Dan is a motorcycle enthusiast and a police buff,
collecting badges and occasionally riding with
detectives in squad cars. What few people know
about Dan Aykroyd is that his right eye is blue and

his left is brown. He is also a victim of syn-
dactylism, a condition where several digits are
fused together. In Dan's case, this affliction affects
his toes. Rather than being ashamed to admit the
abnormality, Dan went to far as to reveal it when
he removed his shoes and socks in the 1979 movie
Mr. Mike's Mondo Video.

He lives with wife Donna and daughters Danielle
Alexandra, born 1989, Kingston Belle, born 1993,
and Stella, born 1998, in their home in the Santa
Monica Mountains near Los Angeles. He usually
spends two months of the year in Ontario.

Dan is also a businessman, investing a substantial part of his movie profits into blues bars, including the Hard Rock Café in Manhattan and Crooks,
a Toronto bar he co-owns with several police offi-
cers. He also expresses his love of blues music by
hosting the nationally syndicated *House of Blues*
radio hour.

Reflecting upon his celebrity status, Dan said to
interviewer Brian D. Johnson of *Maclean's* magazine: "Frankly, I wish I had the money and not
the fame. I can't understand a guy like Donald
Trump. He's got all the money in the world but
still loves the high profile. I don't believe in low
profile. I believe in no profile."

Despite Dan Aykroyd's intentions, his talent and
versatility will keep him a high profile for screen
audiences for a long time to come.

CHAPTER FIVE

Keanu Reeves
(1964–)

KEANU REEVES HAS BECOME A LEADING MAN IN THE TRUEST sense, yet he shares with Mike Myers and Kiefer Sutherland an eclectic preference in his choice of film projects. He has taken roles that added questionable credentials to his motion picture resume while rejecting roles that would have furthered his cinematic profile.

Initially, critics did not take Keanu Reeves seriously. He was often described as "wooden" and not a performer of deep roles. Early in his career he was given roles that projected him as a "talent" of limited range and intelligence—a dark-haired surfer boy whose vocabulary was mostly limited to referring to his peers as "dude."

While these parts brought him public attention, he quickly proved his mettle and was soon working alongside some of the greatest actors in the industry, including Gene Hackman, Denzel Washington and Anthony Hopkins. He was even given the exalted privilege of top billing over Al Pacino in *The Devil's Advocate* (1997). And he has had the good fortune to be directed by many of the top names in the business, such as Bernardo Bertolucci, Francis Ford Coppola, Kenneth Branagh and Lawrence Kasdan.

Constantine (2005)

Keanu is the master of his destiny. Professionally and personally, he is his own man and refuses to capitulate to his movie star status. For example, he has adopted the Buddhist religion as his philosophy. Despite his superstar salaries, he did not buy a house for many years, instead living an almost nomadic existence in various hotel suites. He is an intensely private man who chooses to express his inner self through his various stage and screen portrayals. He works to entertain his audience, but he also selects his film roles to heighten his creative identity.

Keanu describes himself as a "middle-class white boy. A bourgeois middle-class white boy with an absent father, a strong-willed mother and two beautiful younger sisters."

Keanu is of Hawaiian heritage. His unusual first name is a combination of *ke* (meaning "the") and *anu* (meaning "cool breeze over the mountains"). He entered the world as Keanu Charles Reeves on September 2, 1964 in Beirut, Lebanon. His father Samuel Nowlin Reeves, a part-Chinese, part-Hawaiian geologist, had married English showgirl Patricia Taylor after watching her perform in a Beirut nightclub.

The family moved to Australia, where Keanu's sister Kim was born, but there unfortunately, the marriage dissolved. Following the divorce, Samuel returned to Hawaii while Patricia and the children moved to New York. It was there that Patricia met and married stage and film director Paul Aaron, and the family moved to Toronto. But this marriage did not survive either. However, unlike Samuel, Aaron continued to "be there" for Keanu after the break-up. As Keanu grew, Patricia married two more times, to rock promoter Robert Miller, whose sports enthusiasms, particularly as a hockey goalie, earned him the title of "The Wall," and to hair-dresser Jack Bond, whom she divorced in 1994.

Keanu, who took up Canadian citizenship, became a great hockey fan. His other passion was drama—though he wasn't the most studious of students. He once remarked: "I'm a meat-headed man. You've got smart people, and you've got dumb people. I just happen to be dumb." A modest comment—and maybe true, but Keanu proved his acting worth through practical application. He had a love for the craft, and at the age of 14, decided to pursue a career in acting.

Keanu made his professional debut in a 1978 CBC TV series called *Hanging In*, a comedy set in a youth counselling centre. He played a tough streetwise kid whose first scene had him saying: "Hey lady, can I use the shower?"

It was not a memorable entrance, but Keanu was cast next as a dancer in a Coca-Cola commercial. He made such an impression with the company that Coke used him again in a 1983 ad where his character's disappointment at losing a bike race is assuaged by his father handing him a Coke.

Soon Keanu's face became a familiar one on high-profile TV commercials, including a spot on a Kellogg's Corn Flakes ad that provided him with his first top-dollar paycheque.

Keanu attended various high schools including the Toronto School for the Performing Arts before dropping out at the age of 17. At that point, he decided to focus his full attention on a film/theatrical career. Despite his TV commercial background, the work did not come looking for him, and Keanu supported himself by taking on such menial jobs as sharpening ice skates and working as a pasta chef (at a restaurant he also managed) and as a landscaper.

He began winning stage roles in such productions as *For Adults Only*, *The Crucible*, and *Romeo and Juliet* (as Mercutio). It was a busy time for Keanu, who also hosted the third season of a kid's TV show, *Going Great* (1982), opposite another Canadian up-and-comer, Megan Follows. In 1984, Keanu played a suicidal teenager in a play called *Wolfboy*, and Keanu was awarded an Equity card for his role in this controversial production. His first film role was in the made-for-TV movie *Letting Go* (1985), a tearjerker about lost relationships starring John Ritter. Keanu played "Stereo Teen #1."

Next on his agenda was a National Film Board of Canada drama called *One Step Away*. Here he played a traditional street punk with a guilty conscience. Then he appeared as the hockey player Heaver in the film *Youngblood* (1986), opposite Rob Lowe and Patrick Swayze. As with most Canadian actors of his generation, Keanu had a passion for hockey and relished the opportunity to display his on-ice abilities onscreen.

His moderate success in *Youngblood* prompted Keanu to try his luck in Hollywood. In 1986, he

left Canada for Los Angeles with $3000 in his
pocket, driving his old Volvo. He found lodgings
with her former stepfather Paul Aaron while he
scouted for movie work. Luckily, he scored a motion
picture role almost immediately, with a role in
the 1986 slacker movie *River's Edge*. This was a
powerful production, based on factual incidents, in
which Keanu plays a character suffering a moral
dilemma after a young woman is killed by his high
school buddy, her boyfriend.

River's Edge, despite its disturbing story line, was
a hit, and suddenly Keanu found himself a hot
Hollywood commodity. However, his manager had
reservations concerning his name, Keanu, which
he thought was too exotic. They settled on "K.C.
Reeves," but that proved a short-lived pseudonym
when Keanu quickly reverted to his original name.

He appeared on screen at least eight times in
1986. He appeared with Charles Bronson in another
true-life story *Act of Vengeance*, in *Young Again*
where a 40-ish Robert Urich is transformed into a
youthful Keanu Reeves; then he portrayed the son
of an alcoholic Andy Griffith in the television
movie *Under the Influence*.

The work continued, including a role in the
remake of the classic *Babes in Toyland*, where he co-
starred with Drew Barrymore. The Canadian-
made *Flying* and a co-starring role alongside Kiefer
Sutherland in *Brotherhood of Justice* followed.

His new profile brought him to the attention of
Oliver Stone, who thought him ideal for the lead
role in his proposed Vietnam picture *Platoon*.

Keanu refused the part because he objected to the film's excessive violence and was replaced by Charlie Sheen.

Keanu instead took a role in the goofy teen comedy *The Night Before* (1988), a forgettable romp where he played Winston Connelly, a high school nerd who, on a bet, finds himself the escort of pretty Lori Loughlin to the senior prom.

Keanu's work at this point was not critically demanding material, although with each role, he honed his craft. He soon required more demanding roles, and the opportunity arose when he appeared in the picture *Permanent Record,* a powerful movie dealing with teenage suicide. Keanu proved a standout as the victim's underachieving friend, who, drunk and guilt-ridden, confronts the suicide victim's father and brother. It is a powerful scene that allowed the young actor the chance to display his dramatic potential.

The Prince of Pennsylvania followed, a quirky comedy where Keanu, replete with a kind of Mohawk haircut, becomes involved in a plot to kidnap his father (Fred Ward) while romancing the older Amy Madigan. None of these films broke box office records, but Keanu was more creatively satisfied with these projects than with his earlier roles.

In *Dangerous Liaisons,* based on the Christopher Hampton play *Les Liaisons Dangereuses*, Keanu took the role of Chevalier Danceny. This was surely his most important and demanding part to date, starring opposite John Malkovich, Glenn Close and Michelle Pfeiffer in a movie directed by Stephen

Frears. Many critics claimed that Keanu (and Malkovich) were miscast in this period piece, but the picture broadened Keanu's cinematic appeal.

He turned down the lead role in *The Fly II* (1989), which was inherited by *Mask*'s Eric Stoltz, whose career was on the downslide. He instead appeared in *Bill and Ted's Excellent Adventure*, where, as Ted Logan, he defined his onscreen persona. The movie features Keanu as a not-so-bright high school student needing to pass his final history assignment, and he is given a time machine. During the filming of the movie, which was described as "equal parts Mark Twain, Monty Python and rock 'n' roll," Reeves and co-star Alex Winter entertained the crew with Monty Python sketches. The movie is a mindless affair, but it became a huge financial success. The picture best succeeded at one thing—enhancing Keanu's visibility. He next appeared in Ron Howard's *Parenthood*, which was not one of the acclaimed director's biggest hits, but Keanu delivered an effective performance in his familiar role as a teenage slacker.

Keanu decided to widen his experience and once again took to the stage, appearing first in Shakespeare's *The Tempest* before taking on a role in the American Playhouse production of *Life Under Water*. It was another interesting role for Keanu, who, though now well into his 20s, was again cast as a moody adolescent, *a la* James Dean.

The casting was not a happy experience for Keanu. While the film was financially profitable for Keanu, it was certainly not creatively fulfilling, and Keanu was still stuck in the mould he had made for himself as Ted. Keanu complained at the time: "If I suddenly died, they would carve 'I played Ted' on my headstone."

He appeared in more adult roles in such movies as *I Love You to Death* (1990) and a cameo in *Tune in Tomorrow*. He was improbably cast as a maverick FBI agent on the trail of bank robber and professional surfer Patrick Swayze in *Point Blank* (1991) before reprising his most audience-proof character in *Bill and Ted's Bogus Journey*.

Following the release of that sequel, Keanu decided to expand his image. He wanted to play stronger, more mature roles, such as the part he played in *My Own Private Idaho*, directed by Gus Van Sant. In this film, he appeared with his pal River Phoenix, who sadly later achieved immortality through his death from a drug overdose. Keanu was devastated by the loss of his best friend, but carried on.

In 1992, Keanu faced his greatest challenge to date. Noted director Francis Ford Coppola required Keanu's services to play Jonathan Harker in his upcoming version of *Bram Stoker's Dracula* (1992), where Keanu would co-star opposite Gary Oldman (as the bloodthirsty Count), Winona Ryder, and Anthony Hopkins, as Professor Van Helsing, the vampire's nemesis.

The movie is stunningly photographed with a sumptuous recreation of the era. Oldman, Ryder and Hopkins are each excellent in their roles. Sadly, it is Keanu who almost sinks the show. His performance of Jonathan Harker was panned as wooden, a common complaint pointed at Keanu by his critics. Criticism of the movie aside, Keanu had proven himself to be a talented and versatile performer.

Undaunted by the critical backlash, Keanu boldly proceeded into his next period piece, the 1993 British production of Shakespeare's *Much Ado About Nothing*, directed by and starring Kenneth Branagh. Once again, Keanu played a supporting part as Don John, an evil character trying to destroy the love affair between Kate Beckinsale and Robert Sean Leonard. Unlike his playing in *Bram Stoker's Dracula,* he seemed comfortable in Shakespearean dramas and gave a credible performance.

Keanu continued along his eclectic creative trek. After his work in *Much Ado About Nothing,* he was seen in a cameo role in *Freaked* (1993). He probably appeared in this picture (where he was billed as Ortiz the Dog Boy) as a favour to his *Bill and Ted* co-star and friend Alex Winter, who was attempting to establish a career as a director. *Freaked* did not have much chance of wide box office appeal, and the movie failed miserably, earning a box office take of less than $30,000. Grosses, though, seemed hardly a point of consideration for Keanu. He chose work based on each role's individual merit and considered himself fortunate that, despite his failures, he was still in demand. Outside of *Bill and Ted's Excellent Adventure*, he hadn't enjoyed a major box office hit. Certainly, such pictures as Bertolucci's *Little Buddha* (1993) where he buffed up his frail frame to essay the part, brought him prestige as an actor, but where were the dollars?

Fortunately, all that was about to change. Director Jan De Bont was preparing an action picture to be called *Speed*. Keanu Reeves was not first on the list to play bomb expert Jack Traven, who spends most of the picture helping a bus passenger (Sandra Bullock) steer an explosives-sabotaged bus through L.A. streets, the bomb planted on the bus by a bomb-expert-gone-bad (Dennis Hopper). A-list actors Tom Hanks, Tom Cruise, Johnny Depp and Bruce Willis had turned down the role of Jack Traven. Apparently, Keanu didn't jump at the part either, but he saw the box office potential of the project and accepted the role. His decision turned out to be the smartest move of Keanu's career. *Speed* placed him as a box office champion, now on a par with the actors who had rejected the part. The film is a non-stop roller coaster ride, and Keanu plays the perfect hero. The film sped all the way to the box office, where it had a huge take.

Speed became not only the title of a movie, but it also described the pace that Keanu Reeves' career was progressing. He was now one of Hollywood's hottest superstars.

Unfortunately, *Johnny Mnemonic* (1995) was an absolutely dreadful follow-up to Keanu's megahit. The picture itself is silly and flat, and his role allows him no depth or emotional range. The movie crashed at the box office.

Still, it wasn't a bad time for Keanu. He continued to receive film offers, and he continued to choose projects that appealed to his artistic sensibilities. He turned down a role in *Heat*, in which he would have appeared opposite Al Pacino and Robert De Niro, to fly to Winnipeg in the dead of winter to play the lead role of *Hamlet* at the Manitoba Theatre Centre.

Fans from as far away as Germany and Australia travelled to Winnipeg to watch him portray the Bard's greatest character. His highest compliment came from the noted Shakespearean actor and director Kenneth Branagh who said of Keanu: "He has the indelible essence called 'star quality.'"

However, local critics were mixed and not generous in their reviews. It was apparent that Keanu's "movie star" reputation provided more prominence to the production than the quality of his rendition of this most challenging role. Keanu had trained for the part by memorizing a worn paperback edition he carried with him while working in L.A. But that was hardly enough preparation for the performance.

Keanu did enjoy a critically regarded role opposite the legendary Anthony Quinn in *A Walk in the Clouds* (1995), but the picture fell flat at the box office. *Chain Reaction* (1996) and *Feeling Minnesota* fared no better. *The Last Time I Committed Suicide* was a complete bomb, earning just $46,362.

It seemed as though Keanu's career was sinking rather than swimming. He'd not been in a commercially successful motion picture since *Speed*, three years earlier. He rejected the chance to reprise his character of Jack Traven, in *Speed 2*. (Former co-star Sandra Bullock appeared in the film to her regret, as the film was a disaster.)

Instead Keanu signed on to the role of attorney Kevin Lomax in *The Devil's Advocate* (1997), a part that Brad Pitt turned down.

In *The Devil's Advocate*, Keanu plays against Al Pacino, who plays the devil and possesses the body of lawyer John Milton (Keanu's boss) and corrupts Milton's already-questionable morals. Canadian Keanu top-billed Pacino—the first time that the latter had not received first billing since *The Godfather* (1972). This was a definite coup for Keanu, as other top-league Pacino co-stars, such as Sean Penn and Johnny Depp, were not awarded marquee consideration over Pacino. Keanu plays his role effectively, if a little blandly, but it is Al Pacino who steals the picture. As with every role he plays, Pacino infuses John Milton with an energy and intensity that simply blows everyone else off the screen. Despite the casting of two superstars (and the addition of Charlize Theron, who plays Keanu's wife), *The Devil's Advocate* failed to catch fire at the box office.

Keanu's next picture was a personal choice—*Me and Will* (1999), a cameo part that he accepted because it afforded him the opportunity to appear onscreen with his band Dogstar. In Dogstar, he plays bass guitar. (The band has gone into hibernation, and Reeves now plays with the rock band becky.) Keanu expressed pride in Dogstar's releasing two album's *Our Little Visionary* in 1996 and *Happy Ending* in 2000.

Keanu scored his biggest hit when he accepted a starring role turned down by Ewan McGregor and Will Smith. *The Matrix* (1999) is a science fiction thriller about a computer hacker named Neo (Reeves) who discovers that the world he thinks he is living in is actually an illusion orchestrated by computers that have taken over the world. Keanu stars with fellow Canadian Carrie-Anne Moss whom he dated during the filming. Filmed in Australia, the picture required Keanu to be in top physical condition for the action scenes. To prepare, Keanu underwent a four-month training period learning martial arts. *The Matrix*, despite a convoluted storyline that at times contradicts itself, proved enormously popular at box offices.

Keanu was rewarded with a $10-million salary, plus a reported 15% of the gross. Professionally this was a happy time for Keanu. But in his personal life, he experienced tragedies. In December 1999, his long-time girlfriend Jennifer Syme delivered a stillborn baby girl, and the following year they broke up. Then in 2001, Jennifer was killed in a car accident on Los Angeles Hwy 101. Keanu remained close to Jennifer's mother during the difficult time, lending support and helping her out financially.

Fortunately, the number of film role offers stayed strong, and Keanu struggled hard to escape the surfer boy image that dogged him. The image got Reeves a role in *The Replacements* (2000), an unfunny football comedy in which he once again receives top billing over an established co-star— this time, Gene Hackman. Keanu gave up some of his fee for this movie so that Hackman could be hired for the colourful role of the football coach.

In his next two pictures, Keanu ventured into darker territories. *The Watcher* provided Keanu with his most malevolent role to date, where he played a woman-preying serial killer being tracked by FBI agent James Spader. Despite the creative opportunity the film afforded him, *The Watcher* was not a film Keanu wanted to make. He'd first accepted the part because it was a small role with interesting character dimensions. Then after Keanu was contractually committed to the picture, his part was enlarged substantially, though his fee remained far beneath the salaries of co-stars James Spader and Marisa Tomei. To try to get out of the film, Keanu claimed a friend forged the signature on the contract. At the end, Keanu made the film and gave a credible and frightening performance.

The Gift was another film that allowed Keanu to expand his talents with a sinister, sociopathic role, in this case as Donnie Barksdale, the abusive husband of Hillary Swank. The movie was written by Billy Bob Thornton and directed by Sam Raimi, famous for his *The Evil Dead* series and later for the *Spider-Man* movies. Keanu delivered another strong performance (he'd consulted counsellors to develop a psychological understanding of his character) and once more proved to his critics that he was an actor of depth and substance. However, neither movie was successful at the box office.

Keanu fared slightly better with his next two film projects. *Sweet November* (2001) was a remake of a 1968 comedy-drama. In this retelling, Keanu played opposite his former *Devil's Advocate* co-star Charlize Theron. Keanu plays an advertising executive involved with a free-spirited soul who enjoys brief involvement with men in order to improve them. The drama in the film begins when it is discovered that the Charlize Theron character is dying.

Hardball presented Keanu as a hard-drinking gambler who agrees to coach a kid's baseball team in the Chicago projects...with predictable results. What makes this picture different from others of its type is that the story is based on the true-life experiences of Daniel Coyle, who wrote the book on which the movie is based. *Hardball* was no hardcore winner, but it placed Keanu on the A-list of Hollywood actors.

Keanu once again found professional success offset by personal difficulties. He was seriously injured in a motorcycle riding accident in Topanga Canyon, outside Los Angeles. He suffered a ruptured spleen, leaving him with a long scar on his abdomen that has plagued him (and makeup crews) in shirtless shots ever since.

He also had family problems. Samuel, Keanu's biological father, estranged from his only son for 25 years, was arrested for selling heroin and given a 10-year sentence. After his release, he faced difficult financial times and lived with Keanu's grandmother, subsisting on food stamps. Keanu was unsympathetic to his father's plight.

Then his sister Kim was diagnosed with leukemia. The two had always been close. Fortunately, he could afford to care for her in the best of comfort and temporarily left the set of *The Matrix* sequel to take her to Hawaii.

Keanu filmed *The Matrix*'s two sequels back to back. *The Matrix Reloaded* (2003) and *The Matrix Revolutions* (2003) continued the adventures of his character Neo and proved to be huge financial successes.

Keanu has a few films scheduled for 2005 release, including *The Night Watchman, A Scanner Darkly, Constantine* and *Thumbsucker.* His talent and efforts have made Keanu Reeves a superstar, despite the fact that he's chosen to buck the odds and play by his own rules.

Keanu is an extremely private man He rarely consents to interviews or publicity—and never uses his personal life to raise his public profile. Keanu Reeves still has Canadian citizenship. His hobbies are motorcycle and horseback riding and surfing.

In 1995, *Esquire* magazine selected him one of "the 100 sexiest actors of all time." He was honoured with a star on The Hollywood Walk of Fame on January 31, 2005.

But these signs of recognition have little significance for Keanu. Polls, awards and even superstar status never appealed to him. This Canadian talent measures his success by the quality of the work. With quality as his motivation, Keanu Reeves dedicates himself to his craft.

CHAPTER SIX

Pamela Anderson
(1967–)

WHILE MOST PEOPLE IN THE ENTERTAINMENT INDUSTRY OFTEN have to work for years or even decades before achieving recognition, there are those (very) rare instances when one is instantly "discovered." "Sweater girl" Lana Turner is probably the most famous example, when she was discovered at the soda fountain of Schwab's Drug Store in Hollywood. Another famous story of "being at the right place at the right time" concerns Canadian-born Pamela Anderson.

Pamela Anderson's great acting ability was eclipsed by her physical attributes that caught viewers' attention and allowed her to enjoy enormous popularity during the 1990s. She has proven herself to be no dumb blonde, despite the proliferation of parts that cast her in that role. She co-produced and starred in the successful *Charlie's Angels*-like TV series *V.I.P.*

Unfortunately, Pamela Anderson has become less known for her acting than for her controversial private life, with attention centring on her breast implants and her relationship with grunge rocker Tommy Lee. Pamela recently announced her decision to retire from show business. When

her career slowed down following the cancellation of *V.I.P.*, she decided to concentrate on being a mom. As she explained in an *E! News Live* interview, "I don't want to be an actress. I never did want to be an actress." Nevertheless, blessed with brains, beauty—and more than a little luck—Pamela Anderson had a good run at it.

Even her entry into the world brought her a claim to fame. Pamela Denise Anderson was born in Ladysmith, BC, on July 1, 1967, which happened to be Canada's 100th Birthday. Her arrival at 4:08 AM made her the first baby born on that day in all of the country. As a result, she was given the title "The Centennial Baby." The event was reported in the local newspaper, *The Ladysmith-Chemainus Chronicle.* Besides the publicity, the Anderson family was given cash prizes and awards.

Shortly after Pamela's birth, the Andersons moved to Comox, BC, where father Barry worked as a furnace repairman and her mother Carol found a job as a waitress. One day, Pamela was sitting in a local library with about 100 other children when a photographer snapped a picture of her. The picture impressed all who saw it, and it was quickly copyrighted and placed in all the libraries in BC.

Except for her early success, Pamela's teen years were uneventful. Although strikingly attractive, she wore braces. She was active in sports and proved herself a natural athlete, excelling at volleyball and earning the nickname "Rubber-Band" for her flexibility. But as her gym teacher later remarked: "There was really nothing special about her."

One of Pamela's hobbies was playing the saxophone, which she enjoyed playing with friends and in the school band. She was also very competitive and tried to better the achievements of her friends and classmates. As her mother Carol later said, "She was very determined."

Still in high school, she appeared in a brief role as a prostitute in the Kathleen Turner/Anthony Perkins *Crimes of Passion* (1984). Pamela graduated from Highland Secondary School in 1985, and she stated for the yearbook that her ambition in life was "To be a California Beach Bum." Just after graduation, she played a party guest in *Some Kind of Wonderful* (1987).

In 1988, Pamela moved to Vancouver, where she found work as a fitness instructor. In the summer of 1989, she was attending a football game between the BC Lions and the Toronto Argonauts with some friends when the cameraman, scanning the crowd for interesting faces, pointed his lens at Pamela and broadcast a picture of her widely smiling face on the stadium's big screen. The stadium went wild. She happened to be wearing a Labatt's T-shirt given to her by one of her friends who worked for that brewing company. This free beer advertisement plus the crowd's reaction to Pamela resulted in her being hired as the "Blue Girl." Pamela posters were quickly tacked up in bars and restaurants across Canada.

It was the second time that Pamela Anderson had been "picked from the crowd."

The campaign proved so successful that Pamela was quickly hired to appear as the model for other advertisements and endorsements. A freelance Vancouver photographer who had taken some shots of Pamela convinced her to let him send the pictures to *Playboy*. Playboy editors responded with definite interest and flew her down to Los Angeles, where her first assignment was as the cover model for the October 1989 issue. Eventually, Pamela Anderson appeared on the cover of *Playboy* five times, more than anyone else in that magazine's history.

The popular cover photo was the real beginning of Pamela's acting career. In 1990 she guest starred as Yvette on the popular Fox program *Married...with Children*, and her appearance was so well received that she was asked back for another guest spot on the show the following year.

The role that really made her mark was that of Lisa, the "Tool Time Girl" on the series *Home Improvement*, where each week she introduced Tim Allen's "Tool Time" program.

The year 1992 was an exciting and productive one for Pamela. David Hasselhoff, the producer and star of the successful *Baywatch* series (which was later touted as the most watched show in the world!) saw Pamela on *Home Improvement* and signed her for the role of California lifeguard C.J. (Casey Jean) Parker. Pamela was eager to play the role—recalling her high school yearbook inscription. She was an immediate hit, especially with the male audience. During the first two years of *Baywatch*, Pamela kept her role as the "Tool Time Girl," but the demands became overwhelming, and she left the show and was replaced by Debbie Dunning.

Pamela managed to fit in a couple of movie parts, appearing in the thrillers *The Taking of Beverly Hills* (1992) and *Snapdragon* (1993), where she played the role of twins: one sane, the other psychotic. Unfortunately, neither film electrified audiences or critics. Pamela returned to her TV chores.

The following year, Pamela appeared in three made-for-television movies. Her character of C.J. Parker was featured in a smallish part in *Baywatch the Movie: Forbidden Paradise* and then she did *Come Die with Me, A Mickey Spillane's Mike Hammer Mystery*, where she played Velda, Hammer's loyal secretary. She also played opposite David Keith in the HBO movie *Raw Justice.*

In 1995, besides reprising her *Baywatch* character of C.J. Parker for a third season, she made two TV movies, *The Evolution of Mr. E.*, based on the H.G. Wells story, in which she played a quirky artist/sculptor and *Naked Souls,* in which she had a sexual role.

In 1995, Pamela began a stormy relationship with Motley Crue drummer Tommy Lee. They met at a New Year's party where the tattooed one walked up to Pamela and began licking her feet. He repeatedly asked for her telephone number, and eventually she relented. But each time they arranged a date, something interfered. When Pamela went on assignment to Cancun, Mexico, Tommy followed her and took her out partying. After four days of non-stop partying, the two married on a beach. Pamela legally became Pamela Anderson-Lee and had a wedding band tattooed on her finger in lieu of a ring. The couple returned to Los Angeles, where Pamela was shown a film script that would star her in her first major motion picture.

The movie was *Barb Wire*. Based on a famous comic character in the comic strip of that name, Barb Wire is a futuristic heroine and crime fighter. Pamela's agent tried to talk her out of accepting the part in the unappealingly simple concept, but the opportunity was too tempting for her to turn down. She knew if *Barb Wire* was successful, it had the potential to spawn a series of sequels, as had *Superman* and *Batman*. Her role in the film required extensive action scenes, so Pamela took on a vigorous workout schedule with the personal trainer who had helped Linda Hamilton get in shape for her athletic work in *Terminator 2: Judgment Day* (1991). While the movie was in production, Pamela did many of her own stunts—though few knew she was pregnant at the time. Sadly, this strenuous activity and the stress from balancing the movie with often 10-hour days on the *Baywatch* set caused Pamela to miscarry. Both she and Tommy were devastated. To add to Pamela's depression, *Barb Wire* proved a dismal failure, with most critics panning the picture and Pamela's performance. Audiences seemed to agree as the movie had poor ticket sales. There would clearly be no *Barb Wire* sequels.

Happily, life was brighter for Pamela and Tommy, when in October 1995 Pamela was pregnant again. In December of that year, on a trip to England sponsored by a vicious British tabloid, *The Sun,* Pamela received international bad press when she playfully but naïvely tried to make a member of the Queen's Guard lose his concentration. When asked to stop, Pamela became obnoxious and refused to leave the scene. The police were summoned, and before Tommy could get her away, the situation snowballed. Tommy later claimed he could have resolved the situation if he'd had time, but the police arrived before that could happen. The only good thing that came from Pamela and Tommy's European visit was a renewing of their wedding vows, which took place in Venice, Italy.

On June 6, 1996, she gave birth to a son named Brandon Thomas. She said she was thrilled at being a mother, especially after the loss of their first child. Sadly, less than a year after the renewal of their wedding vows and only five months after Brandon's birth, Pamela filed for divorce from Tommy on November 19, 1996, claiming spousal and child abuse. Allegedly, he had waved a gun threateningly at Pamela and the baby. The divorce was granted, and Pamela officially changed her name back to Pamela Anderson.

The couple reconciled, and hoping that Tommy would successfully deal with his problems, they married again. On December 29, 1997, they had another son, named Dylan. However, the difficulties persisted, and the couple divorced again. Since then she has been linked to German model Marcus Schenkenberg, then was later engaged to rock musician Kid Rock.

One highly publicized incident to arise from the union between Pamela and Tommy Lee occurred when a pornographic home video of the two was stolen from their house and was later distributed by an Internet company. Pamela sued the firm and reportedly settled the case for a reported $10 million.

The breakup of her second marriage to Tommy proved a difficult time for Pamela, but she had her work and her children to keep her occupied. In 1998, she ventured again into TV, as star and co-producer of *V.I.P.*, where she played Vallery Irons, a hot dog stand waitress who is regarded as a hero when she, by accident, saves the life of a movie star. As a result of the publicity, Vallery is hired to become the figurehead of an elite bodyguard agency made up of five experts in espionage and martial arts. The program was typical action fare, but audiences enjoyed its silly premise enough for *V.I.P.* to enjoy a four-season run before ending in May 2002.

In March 2001, Pamela endured more unwanted publicity when a woman named Christine Evelyn Roth was found sleeping in a guest room at Pamela's house. She was deported back to her home country after being charged with trespassing and not the more serious crime of stalking.

Shortly before the sets closed on *V.I.P.*, Pamela publicly disclosed that she had contracted the Hepatitis C virus. She claimed she had acquired the disease from ex-husband Tommy Lee when they allegedly shared the same tattoo needle. Lee denied having the disease and insisted it was a ploy to gain complete custody of their children.

In an October 2003 broadcast of "shock jock," Howard Stern's radio program, Pamela joked that because of her illness she did not expect to live more than 10 to 15 years. This sensational statement put her name in the papers again, and once again, Pamela found her name spread across the tabloid headlines.

While dealing with these difficulties, Pamela returned to movies, but it seemed as if her star had fallen. She was reduced to playing cameo roles in such mindless (but admittedly profitable) films as *Scooby Doo* (2002) and *Scary Movie 3* (2003). She had a minor comeback when she provided the voice for, and co-produced with Stan Lee, the animated cartoon *Stripperella*, a character also created by Lee.

Pamela officially announced her retirement from acting in 2002, saying she wanted to spend more time with her sons. But since then she has changed her mind and announced she is planning to star in an unnamed situation comedy. It has also been announced that she will once again play

C.J. Parker in a big-screen *Baywatch* movie to be produced by Steven Spielberg's DreamWorks.

Acting is not her only business interest. In association with another company, she is developing some licensing ventures that will include clothing, jewellery, accessories and beauty products. The former *Baywatch* babe has recently inked a multibook deal with Simon and Shuster.

Then there are her personal passions, including building schools for underprivileged children throughout the world and offering support to women who have come from abusive situations. Her philanthropic endeavours have presented her with many honours, including a humanitarian award presented to her from Sir Paul McCartney for her work with PETA (People for the Ethical Treatment of Animals).

Her most recent work in furthering this cause is a billboard advertising campaign in China that shows a partially clad Pamela expressing her disapproval over the slaughter of animals for the manufacture of outerwear clothing. She was quoted as saying, "I'm perfectly happy to bare my skin if it will help to save animal skins. With so many fashionable and comfortable fur alternatives available today, there is no excuse for killing animals and stealing their skins." Naturally, the campaign is producing headaches for censors in China. A PETA spokesperson said, in order to get approval to display the ads, it might be necessary to trim the pictures.

It seems apparent that Pamela has not been slowed by her diagnosis of Hepatitis C. Instead, she's become more active. In her appointment as the celebrity spokesperson for the American Liver Foundation, she's taken on the responsibility of creating public service announcements to generate worldwide awareness of the disease. She also served as the Grand Marshal of the SOS motorcycle fundraiser.

Pamela is proud of her Canadian heritage. Although she gained American citizenship on May 12, 2004, she retains her Canadian citizenship.

In addition to her modelling and acting successes, Pamela Anderson has proven herself a kind, generous and courageous person and a fine role model.

CHAPTER SEVEN

Brendan Fraser
(1968–)

I SEEMS THAT ONE OF THE CONSISTENT ENDEARING QUALITIES of Canadian actors is their penchant for oddball movie roles. Leslie Nielsen, for one, fits this mould. Nielsen achieved prominence as a serious actor in such films as *Forbidden Planet* (1956), *Harlow* (1965) and *The Poseidon Adventure* (1972), but his goofy personality led to the creation of unique comic characters in his later films, including the frantically funny *Airplane!* (1980) and *The Naked Gun* series.

Does Brendan Fraser fit into this equation? The answer is…"yes, completely." He, too, walks the fine line between comedy and drama. While known for his silly antics in live-action versions of popular, vintage cartoon shows, he has also proven himself an actor of power and substance. Brendan projects a recognizable and identifiable vulnerability. While noted primarily for his depiction of characters possessed of heroic qualities, he remains consistently fallible. Of course we know that he will defeat the villain, but we suspect he succeeds only because of luck and possibly even happenstance.

Another trait that has endeared Brendan to his audiences is his likeability. He comes across

onscreen as a genuinely nice guy, a fellow who is approachable. And people relate to that—more so than they relate to an actor like Robert De Niro.

Brendan Fraser has not yet established himself as an actor of the highest commercial potential, but his versatility shines through in each of his roles. The opportunity for movie superstardom still exists for this solid and skilful performer.

Brendan James Fraser was born in Indianapolis, Indiana on December 3, 1968. He comes from a family of sports participants and has an athletic height of 1.9 metres. His Uncle George won a gold medal at the 1952 Helsinki Olympics. His parents, Peter and Carol G. Fraser, are of Canadian descent, but Brendan's early childhood could best be described as nomadic, with travels that took him and his elder siblings Regan, Sean and Kevin throughout the world. By the age of 13, Brendan had lived in London, Rome, Switzerland and various North American cities.

It was while living in London that Brendan discovered a love of acting. While watching a West End matinee of the musical *Oliver!*, he became completely absorbed. When his family lived near Seattle, Washington, Brendan joined the chorus of his school's production of the Rodgers and Hammerstein's musical hit *Oklahoma!*

Later, he played Captain Corcoran in another musical, Gilbert and Sullivan's *H.M.S. Pinafore*. Brendan said he had a turning point in his appreciation of the craft at this time, recalling an evening performance where he accentuated his entrance by grandly tossing his cape high into the air, only to have it drop back onto his head. The people in the audience erupted into laughter, and Brendan, disregarding their amusement, carried on with the scene, at that moment discovering the value of concentration and improvisation.

At 13, Brendan was enrolled in Upper Canada College in Toronto, a prestigious boarding school. While Brendan's grades did not rank him a scholar, he excelled in theatre.

Brendan and his family returned to Seattle following his father's decision to leave his Tourism Canada job. However, Brendan's studies did not suffer, as the boy enrolled in the Cornish College of the Arts. Here, he was influenced by the pantomime expert Bill Irwin, who had appeared in such films as Robert Altman's *Popeye* (1980). Catching an Irwin performance in *The Regard of Flight*, Brendan decided that he wanted to be an actor, in Irwin's style—best described as delivering a total physical performance. His acting has also been inspired by the great Canadian actor Buster Keaton, who is his cinematic hero.

Upon graduating from Cornish with a Bachelor of Fine Arts degree, he took a yearlong internship at the Intiman Theatre and also performed with the Laughing Horse Summer Theatre. By this time, Brendan had earned an impressive package of credentials, including roles in such classical productions as *Romeo and Juliet*, *A Midsummer Night's Dream* and *The Madwoman of Chaillot*.

Brendan auditioned for the part of a Latino in a film called *Bound by Honor*, which was never made. The casting director, Sharon Bialy, didn't think that Brendan was right for the part, but she was impressed with his reading and invited him to visit her office if he ever came to Los Angeles. So after receiving a Masters of Fine Arts degree at the Southern Methodist University in Dallas, Brendan borrowed his mother's car and decided to see if he could succeed in the motion picture business in Los Angeles.

Right from the start he found success in pictures, even though artistically he thumbed his nose at the industry, preferring to remain true to the theatre. But Brendan seemed a natural for films. His first movie was *Dogfight* (1991), where (billed as Brendon Fraser) he appeared opposite Lili Taylor and the tragic River Phoenix. The story concerned a group of marines stationed in San Francisco who, prior to their departure to Vietnam, stage a competition to see who can bring the ugliest girl to a party. Brendan's part as a sailor was brief. He only had one line, but it was an effective movie entrance: "How would you like to eat my s***?" This was not exactly *Casablanca* dialogue, but it fit the part. And, more importantly, the role brought Brendan to the attention of film producers.

Even with this leg-up, Brendan found he still had to pay his dues. Rather than appearing in prestigious A-pictures, he made the rounds of TV movies, such as *Child of Darkness, Child of Light* and *Guilty until Proven Innocent*, where he played Bobby McLaughlin, the troubled adopted son of Harold and Mary

Hohne (Martin Sheen and Caroline Kava). Brendan delivered a powerful performance as an innocent man charged with murder, first having to convince his father of his innocence and then defending himself against his prosecutors. He appeared in one other TV project, *My Old School,* before beginning to make inroads into motion pictures.

His first movie was *Encino Man* (1992), where he appeared as Linkovitch Chomofsky ("Link"), a dormant caveman discovered by Sean Astin and Pauly Shore in Astin's suburban backyard. He wakes up and attempts to adapt to modern California culture. *Encino Man* was not a promising movie debut for an actor hoping to embark on a classical stage career. But despite its goofy premise, *Encino Man* proved popular at the box office.

Brendan also received good notices, such as the brief review featured in *Leonard Maltin's Movie Guide,* where it is noted that "good-natured Brendan (as the cave dude) has his moments." This was not high praise, but at least he scored higher marks than the film itself.

In his next movie, *School Ties,* Brendan played opposite Matt Damon and Chris O'Donnell as a working-class Jewish boy who receives a football scholarship to a college where he becomes the victim of anti-Semitism. Despite its promising premise, the movie doesn't succeed, although Brendan delivers a convincing performance, considering he isn't Jewish.

Brendan's next movie roles didn't offer much promise either. In audience's mind he was still associated with *Encino Man*, and he had to find a way to break out of the mould. He fared a little better in *Twenty Bucks* (1993), a film with an intriguing premise borrowed from the 1943 movie's *Flesh and Fantasy*. The picture revolves around a $20 bill as it goes from hand to hand and the difference it makes to the people who have it.

Brendan seemed committed to pursuing the eclectic in his choices of movie roles. *With Honors* (1994), where he played opposite Joe Pesci, promised much but delivered little in a slight story. Brendan plays Harvard student character Monty Kessler whose thesis falls into the hands of Pesci's character, who uses it to control him.

Despite these artistic compromises, Brendan had become a popular film actor and was in demand. He was up for the role of Charles Van Doren in *Quiz Show* (a role inherited by Ralph Fiennes), but turned down the part because he resented that the film's director Robert Redford had rejected him for the part eventually played by Brad Pitt in *A River Runs Through It* (1992).

Brendan's film choices were still open to question—at least from a commercial standpoint. In *Airheads*, he played Chazz, leader of the rock group The Lone Rangers, who, along with fellow band members (played by Steve Buscemi and Adam Sandler), hold up their local radio station with toy guns to get airplay for their demo tape, appropriately named "Degenerated." Even a co-starring role by veteran actor Joe Mantegna couldn't save this film.

Brendan's next role saw him unbilled in *Now and Then* (1995), which has been described as the female version of the Rob Reiner/Stephen King combination *Stand by Me* (1986). In the film, four friends reminisce at a baby shower about their last summer of adolescence in 1970. Brendan has a brief role as a Vietnam War veteran.

A film in which Brendan definitely made a strong impression was *The Passion of Darkly Noon* (1995), a little-seen independent production in which he co-starred opposite Ashley Judd and Viggo Mortensen. The picture gave Brendan his first real dramatic movie role, as a man torn between his religious beliefs and love for the married Judd.

Another film that allowed Brendan to stretch his talents was the Richard Benjamin-directed *Mrs. Winterbourne*. The movie proved an excellent showcase for Brendan as he played two roles, the two sons of the title character, played by Shirley MacLaine. Brendan also acted with another superstar, Faye Dunaway, in the TV movie *The Twilight of the Golds* (1997). This film gives Brendan a strong role as the gay son of Dunaway and Garry Marshall.

Despite Brendan's impressive credentials, he lost out to Dermot Mulroney for a key part in *My Best Friend's Wedding*, opposite Julia Roberts, but he landed back on his feet with a wallop when he landed the starring role in Disney's *George of the Jungle*. This live-action production was based on the ridiculous antics of Jay Ward's crudely animated cartoon.

Despite the picture's hit-and-miss comic devices, it proved popular box office, mainly thanks to likeable performances by Brendan, co-star Leslie Mann and the wisecracking ape named Ape. It turned in an amazingly large gross. It was all great fun and financially rewarding for Brendan, but it was a goofy role, and he was beginning to worry about becoming typecast.

He need not have been concerned. The time came for him to exploit all of his dramatic potential when he was cast as Clayton Boone in *Gods and Monsters* (1998), a part he got after Robert Downey Jr. rejected the role. Acting opposite the great Ian McKellen in a semi-fictional biopic of the last days of *Frankenstein* (1931) director James Whale, Brendan portrayed his most complicated character to date. *Gods and Monsters* was a success with the critics, but poorly supported by audiences. Brendan was not disappointed with the box office returns. He felt he'd held his own in every scene where he worked with the classically trained McKellen.

1998 saw Brendan earn his first major film award as Best Actor at the Seattle International Film Festival for his work in the sweet romance *Still Breathing*.

On the personal front, on September 27, 1998 Brendan married his long-time girlfriend, Afton Smith, herself an actress who had appeared in small roles in such pictures as *Less Than Zero* (1987) and *Fried Green Tomatoes* (1991). The two share the same birth date, although Afton is one year older than Brendan.

Their first child, a son named Griffin Arthur Fraser, was born on September 17, 2002, followed by Holden Fletcher, on August 16, 2004.

Back at work, Brendan chose another film role that, while not providing the actor with intense dramatic opportunities, allowed him the chance to explore his comedic dimensions. *Blast from the Past* (1999) cast him as Adam Webber, the son of a paranoid inventor (Christopher Walken) who after 35 years locked away in a bomb shelter must deal with modern Los Angeles society. Brendan excelled at the role in which he was typecast—a charming, resourceful but often-incompetent character.

All three of these characteristics came into play when Brendan burst onto the scene as the hero, Rick O'Connell, in Stephen Sommer's *The Mummy*. This role, where he played a character who was flawed and goofy, established beyond recall the Brendan Fraser image. All the work Brendan had done earlier coalesced into the perfect Brendan Fraser performance. O'Connell could best be described as a vulnerable version of Harrison Ford's Indiana Jones. The Universal film, which bore virtually no resemblance to the classic 1932 Boris Karloff film it was based on, was a box office smash and brought in a worldwide gross of $414 million.

Inexplicably, while riding the crest of this movie triumph, Brendan again decided to have another go at a vintage TV cartoon character. It's possible that his reason for accepting the role of *Dudley Do-Right*, "the pride of the Canadian Mounties," was because his great-great-grandfather had served with distinction as a Mounted Police officer.

Brendan braved the lead role but ultimately the part and the movie, released at a short 77-minute length, fell flat. Despite co-starring appearances by Sarah Jessica Parker (as Nell Fenwick) and Alfred Molina as the wonderfully sinister Snidely Whiplash, critical response was brutal. This was reflected in low box office returns. Brendan was disappointed at the poor response to the movie, but he said it was the quality of his work that was important.

In 2000 and 2001, he took on a voice-over role in *Sinbad: Beyond the Veil of Mists*, then appeared in two pictures that seemed to contradict his mandate of "quality work." *Bedazzled* and *Monkeybone* were pictures of little critical and commercial distinction.

Then Brendan again set movie screens ablaze when he reprised his role of Rick O'Connell in *The Mummy Returns* (2001). The movie had a much larger budget, and every dollar was reflected on the screen. It was worth it as the profits from this picture exceeded the returns of the first movie, bringing in an astounding $430 million. The film was the biggest financial success yet for Brendan.

More in line with Brendan's dramatic sensibilities was his next role in *The Quiet American* (2002). This was a powerful part, where Brendan successfully pitted his acting strength against that of the formidable Michael Caine. As Alden Pyle, Brendan turned in his most complex character to date, delivering a multi-layered performance that shattered critics and audiences who still thought he could not perform beyond the minimal demands of *Encino Man*.

Despite his status in the industry, Brendan is not afraid to tackle challenges, including lending his voice to TV narration in *Mummies: The Real Story* (1999), or appearing in and supplying his vocal talents to the 2003 feature *Looney Tunes: Back in Action*.

He's returned to his most famous role, Rick O'Connell, in the third instalment of the Imhotep series *Revenge of the Mummy: The Ride* (2004), for which he received a paycheque of $12.5 million.

Upcoming pictures on Brendan's agenda include *Crash*, *Accidental Husband* and *Singularity*, which are expected to be released in 2005, and another animated voice-over for *Big Bug Man* (expected in 2006).

Brendan's personal passions are travel, culture and photography. He also collects antique Polaroid cameras. His movie successes provide the funds to indulge in these pleasures.

Brendan takes his huge success philosophically. "I believe you have a responsibility to comport yourself in a manner that gives an example to others. As a young man, I prayed for success. Now I pray just to be worthy of it."

There is no way of telling where Brendan Fraser's career will lead him, because Brendan himself doesn't know. He's never had a clear direction as is shown by his choice of roles. It is best to say that he will put his trust in the trails as they open to him. We can be assured that whether playing goofy or serious, Brendan will always give us solid entertainment.

CHAPTER EIGHT

Kiefer Sutherland
(1966–)

IT'S A HOLLYWOOD TRUISM THAT CHILDREN OF FAMOUS parents have a difficult time following in their footsteps. For example, Lon Chaney Jr. and Frank Sinatra Jr., although enjoying respectable careers, never reached the heights attained by their famous fathers. There are countless examples of children of celebrities who failed to establish any kind of acting career. On the other hand, there are also cases of children not only matching their parents' achievements, but also surpassing them. This latter list includes Jane Fonda, Michael Douglas…and Kiefer Sutherland.

At less than 40 years of age, Kiefer has already assembled an impressive resume, both as an actor and director. In the former category, he has delivered sterling performances in all film genres, from drama to horror to comedy. Behind the camera, he has received critical kudos for his directorial accomplishments in such pictures as *Truth or Consequences, N.M.* (1997) and the TV movie *Last Light* (1993).

Given his strong theatrical pedigree, it is not surprising that Kiefer chose a career in the industry. His parents, Donald Sutherland and Shirley Douglas, had established acting careers prior to the

December 21, 1966 birth of Kiefer William Frederick Dempsey George Rufus Sutherland, followed seven minutes later by his twin sister Rachel. She and Kiefer, being twins, are exceptionally close. She, too, works in the television industry as a post-production supervisor in Toronto.

An accomplished actress, Shirley is the daughter of Tommy Douglas, leader of the first socialist government elected in North America. As premier of Saskatchewan from 1944–66, Tommy Douglas is recognized as the founder of Canada's Medicare system. At that time, Kiefer's father Donald had just begun to achieve prominence in the motion picture industry.

Kiefer was born not in Canada but in the United Kingdom, where Donald was working as a film actor and appearing in such British horrors as *Dr. Terror's House of Horrors* (1965) and *Die! Die! My Darling*. Kiefer was named after screenwriter Lorenzo Sabatini (aka Warren Kiefer) who wrote Donald's feature film debut *Castle of the Living Dead* (1964), in which Donald portrayed two roles—one being a witch—opposite Christopher Lee.

Donald and Shirley divorced when Kiefer was four, and the boy moved with his mother from their home in Los Angeles back to Toronto. Kiefer, however, was fortunate to learn the various intricacies of professional acting by spending time with his mother on her Toronto theatre sets and with his father on L.A. movie locations.

Kiefer attended Martingrove Collegiate Institute in Etobicoke, Ontario, but at the age of 15, he decided to become an actor. Rather than stepping directly into the limelight, he began appearing in various youth theatre productions in Toronto, where he quickly established a reputation as an actor of depth.

His performances soon brought Kiefer to the attention of filmmakers, and he made his debut in *Max Dugan Returns* (1983), where he shared screen time with his father. His portrayal in that film so impressed director Daniel Petrie that he cast Kiefer opposite Liv Ullmann in the 1984 Canadian-French co-production *The Bay Boy*.

While the picture did not receive critical or financial recognition, Kiefer was awarded a Genie (Canada's equivalent to an Oscar) for his perform-ance in the film, after which he moved to Los Angeles to further his career. Kiefer was deter-mined to make things happen without his father's assistance, and in short order, he appeared in a small part as one of Sean Penn's cohorts-in-crime in *At Close Range* (1986).

He then enjoyed his first substantial role as the tough punk Ace Merrill in the coming-of-age film *Stand by Me* (1986). Kiefer was effective in the movie, and he displayed a dedication to his craft by remaining in character throughout the shoot, maintaining a brutish behaviour towards co-play-ers Wil Wheaton, River Phoenix, Corey Feldman and Jerry O'Connell even when the cameras weren't rolling. *Stand by Me* was based on Stephen

King's semi-autobiographical novella, *The Body*, and is the most highly regarded of King's print-to-screen offerings, getting both positive critical reviews and healthy box office sales.

Kiefer Sutherland was definitely on a roll. Following *Stand by Me*, he was cast as the lead vampire David in *The Lost Boys* (1987), a moderate success, after which he appeared in *The Killing Time*, where he met and married his co-star, actress Camelia Kath. Their union produced a daughter, Sarah Jude (named after Sarah Jessica Parker and singer/songwriter/composer Jude Cole), but the marriage ended after only two years.

Kiefer was candid when he explained to the press the reason for his failed marriage. "I had an incredible desire at a very young age to want to be older than I was. And one of the ways to accomplish that is to say, 'I'm married; I have kids. I have arrived!' But I found out those aren't the right reasons to do that. Our marriage didn't work out, but we have a beautiful daughter, and I'm very fortunate that Camelia and I have ended up remaining friends."

Kiefer continued to be in demand and appeared in many big-budget hits including *Bright Lights, Big City* (1988), where he acted opposite fellow Canadian Michael J. Fox. Kiefer was a standout as Fox's sleazy, druggy friend Tad Aligash. In *Young Guns*, as gunslinger Josiah Gordon "Doc" Scurlock, Kiefer held his own against contemporaries Emilio Estevez, Charlie Sheen and Lou Diamond Phillips.

Kiefer's appearance in *Young Guns* not only gave him widespread fame, but also provided the young actor with notoriety as part of Hollywood's "brat pack." Kiefer embraced this labelling by gaining tabloid publicity through aggressive and drunken behaviour in public. One of Kiefer's most embarrassing incidents occurred when he was a passenger in Gary Oldman's car when the *JFK* star was arrested for drunken driving in 1991.

But none of these incidents damaged his career. He agreed to recreate his role as "Doc" Scurlock in *Young Guns II* (1990). Although a sequel, the picture came close to the box office power of the first movie. In 1990, he took on the role of Nelson in *Flatliners*. The movie saw him play opposite Kevin Bacon, William Baldwin, Oliver Platt...and Julia Roberts. By the time the picture was released, Kiefer and Julia were in a high-profile romance with marriage preparations scheduled for the summer of 1991. These plans came to naught three days before the expected nuptials when Julia unexpectedly backed out.

At the same time as this tremendous disappointment, Kiefer's film offers slowed down. "I wasn't prepared when the work came to an abrupt stop. I had a chip on my shoulder, and it was getting pretty heavy," he later said.

But it wasn't long before Kiefer resumed his career with strong supporting roles in Rob Reiner's *A Few Good Men* (1992), where he played Lieutenant Jonathan Kendrick, and was part of a stellar cast that included Tom Cruise, Jack Nicholson,

Kevin Bacon and Demi Moore. The film was a good showcase for Kiefer and proved a box office smash.

He next appeared in another "brat pack" feature, this one based on the Alexander Dumas classic *The Three Musketeers* (1993), in which he starred with Charlie Sheen, Demi Moore and Chris O'Donnell.

Shortly after completing the picture, Kiefer escaped from Hollywood and the destructive lifestyle he was living there to spend time on his 400-hectare ranch in Montana. He spent his time perfecting his rodeo riding skills.

Kiefer had an impressive portfolio of film work, including roles in *Article 99* (1992), where he paid tribute to his dad's role as "Hawkeye" Pierce in the 1970 movie *M*A*S*H* by wearing the same eyeglasses and fishing hat that his father had worn. He then did a small role as FBI Agent Sam Stanley in *Twin Peaks: Fire Walk with Me*, a film based on David Lynch's quirky television series *Twin Peaks*.

Kiefer publicly didn't have any praise for the movies he was doing at this time. He was quoted as saying: "I needed to take time off. I was doing awful films and just needed to stop. You need the money, your kids have to go to school—you start justifying it. I was doing really sh**** work, which I only blame myself for. And I needed to stop and figure out what I was doing with my life."

The talented Kiefer soon found a new way to use his creative energies when he took on his first directing assignment on the critically acclaimed TV offering *Last Light* (1993), where he appeared as death row inmate Denver Bayliss, opposite Forest Whitaker as the prison guard he befriends. Kiefer's low-key direction earned the picture several Cable Ace nominations.

One of the most powerful roles Kiefer has played was as Jeff Harriman in the 1993 remake of the French-Dutch classic *The Vanishing,* a case of reverse role-casting where "bad guy" actor Kiefer plays the hero and "good guy" actor Jeff Bridges plays the villain. In the movie, Kiefer is the boyfriend of Nancy Travis, who is abducted by Bridges.

Kiefer worked in a variety of films, including *The Cowboy Way* (1994) opposite Woody Harrelson and *A Time to Kill* (1996). He returned to directing in 1997 with the crime thriller *Truth or Consequences, N.M.*, in which he also plays the role of Ku Klux Klan redneck Curtis Freley. Sadly, this film proved poison at the box office.

More satisfying to Kiefer was the opportunity to play opposite his mother in the 1997 stage production of Tennessee William's *The Glass Menagerie*, performed at the Royal Alexandra Theatre in Toronto.

On the film set, however, Kiefer continued to enjoy playing the bad guy. He excelled in such portrayals as the child-killer/rapist in *An Eye for an Eye* (1996) where his character Robert Doob brutally assaults the daughter of Sally Field, leading her into a vendetta of revenge against her attacker. He built upon his villainous reputation by playing the psychotic child psychiatrist in *Freeway,* co-starring Reese Witherspoon.

Kiefer was unhappy with his film work and escaped from Hollywood to compete on the rodeo circuit. Kiefer and his partner John English won several rodeo competitions, including the 1998 U.S. Team Roping Championships. Kiefer remembered, "I was as shocked as anyone when we won our first rodeo. But I'm a competitive person. I wanted that buckle. But that wasn't the reason why I did it. I just really enjoyed the whole process, the discipline and the whole experience."

He married fellow Torontonian Kelly Wynn, a model, on June 24, 1996, but they stayed together only four years, divorcing in 2000.

After the wedding, he took a hiatus from moviemaking, but Kiefer remained an actor at heart and before long he began to miss performing. "I remembered the great times I had making films," he recalled. "And how lucky I was to have been in that position in the first place."

There was no lack of work for Kiefer, but the quality of his projects was not outstanding. He appeared with Dennis Hopper (with whom he'd worked in 1990s *Flashback*) in a poorly received *Pulp Fiction* wannabe, *The Last Days of Frankie the Fly* (1997). He acted in four films in 1998, but only one, the bleak science fiction thriller *Dark City*, was semi-successful in the theatres. The others, *A Soldier's Sweetheart*, *Break Up* and *Ground Control*, went straight to video shelves. Unfortunately, one of Kiefer's most effective performances was in another film few saw. He played writer William S. Burroughs in *Beat* (2000).

Kiefer fared no better when he returned to directing and helmed *Woman Wanted* (2000), filmed in Winnipeg. Despite fine acting by Holly Hunter, the film was a total misfire. Kiefer insisted that his name as director be removed from the credits and be replaced with "Allan Smithee." His name appeared in the credits as an actor for his role as Wendell Goddard.

Kiefer returned to acting, although the films in which he appeared didn't improve. *Picking Up the Pieces* was a black comedy that was far from classic Woody Allen, but Kiefer was pleased to work with the eccentric, brilliant director. In 2001, Kiefer made *Cowboy Up* and the intriguingly titled *To End All Wars*. And 2002 saw him in *Desert Saints*, *Dead Heat* and *Behind the Red Door*. It is doubtful if any of these films were shown in theatres before their video release.

Dissatisfaction with his movie career prompted Kiefer to accept a role in a weekly television series. This series, entitled *24*, appealed to him because it was not a sitcom nor was it a hospital or police procedural drama. It was a program with a distinctive difference. This difference was a device that was expected to keep viewers watching week after week. And it worked! The series was shot in real time over 24 weeks, with each episode representing an hour of the story. Kiefer plays Jack Bauer, a counterterrorism agent who races against the clock to prevent disasters—assassinations, nuclear explosions and so on. In the first season, he had to prevent a presidential candidate's assassination and rescue the candidate's kidnapped daughter, at the same time dealing with his own domestic troubles. The series is an enormous success with critics and audiences alike, earning Kiefer a well-deserved Golden Globe for best actor in a dramatic series. Upon receiving his award, the overjoyed Kiefer commented: "I've lost all feeling in my lower half."

The series *24* is one of television's most critically acclaimed series. It is a combination of sharp writing and superb direction. Describing the show, Kiefer said: "I have watched over the last five years a huge transition—shows like *The West Wing*, *ER* and *The Sopranos*—a lot of programming on television which was better than a lot of movies I was seeing. It was certainly better than most of the movies I was, in fact, making. From that perspective, if you're trying something you think is interesting, new and fresh, the stigma of swapping medium is not nearly what it used to be, certainly when I started. I was very, very lucky."

As of this writing, *24* is midway through Season Four, and chances are good it will have a fifth season.

Despite his series' success, Kiefer had not abandoned films entirely; he has simply balanced his movie roles with his television obligations. In 2004, Kiefer appeared in a movie called *Taking Lives*. This gruesome film based on the novel by Michael Pye afforded Kiefer top billing opposite Ethan Hawke and Angelina Jolie, even though his character is on screen for less than three minutes.

Kiefer has a distinctive baritone, and he began doing voice work in such animated features as *The Nutcracker Prince* (1990) and also provided the vocal talent for *The Land Before Time X: The Great Longneck Migration* (2003). Kiefer's voice was never better used than as The Caller in 2002's *Phone Booth*. Here Kiefer created a chilling portrayal of a psychopathic stalker condemning an innocent man (Colin Farrell) to a period of hell trapped within the confines of a Manhattan phone booth.

There appears to be no end to Kiefer Sutherland's versatility. In the TV series *Watership Down* (1999), he provided the voice of Hickory; in *Paradise Found* (2003), he played artist Paul Gauguin. Keifer is not afraid to take chances.

Regarding his reputation as one of the screen's quintessential bad guys, Kiefer remarked, "When you're a young actor you like to go for characters with a bit of flair. So in many of the films I've done, I ended up playing weirdos. But I can assure you, I'm not a psycho or a criminal or a bully." It is his versatility that allows him to play such roles convincingly.

Kiefer has bridged the gap between film and television and is also recognized for his talents as a director. What is amazing is that Kiefer has accomplished this before reaching the age of 40! Despite this output of work, Kiefer Sutherland is modest and regards himself more as a journeyman actor than a bona fide star. Discussing his career, Kiefer has been quoted as saying: "I'm not on everybody's first list to do bigger films."

Kiefer continues to work hard at his craft. For his role in *The Wild*, which is scheduled for a 2006 release, he had to practice roaring like a lion. Kiefer chose to practice growling while commuting on the freeway. His mouthy facial expressions were often noticed by other drivers, most of whom did not recognize the actor spouting his lines.

Kiefer spent the summer of 2004 in New Zealand filming the epic period drama, *River Queen*, scheduled for a December 2005 release.

Noted film critic Leonard Maltin provides a good summation of Kiefer Sutherland in his classic *Movie Encyclopedia*: "The spitting image of his father, Donald Sutherland, this young, square-faced actor seems due for major success....He handles starring roles and supporting parts equally well, and to date he's avoided typecasting."

Kiefer Sutherland chooses not to be on Hollywood's A-list. As things are now, he has a high enough profile to be guaranteed work while still pursuing his own direction in the industry.

CHAPTER NINE

Carrie-Anne Moss
(1967–)

CARRIE-ANNE MOSS FIRST MADE AN IMPACT WITH MOVIE audiences in her role as Trinity in *The Matrix* (1999). This star-making part is only one of many interesting and unique characters Carrie-Anne has played. A versatile actress, Carrie-Anne has played roles on television and in films and is best known for portraying strong characters. Carrie-Anne Moss is not known for romantic, comedic or fluffy roles. She is an action heroine, in the same vein as *The Terminator*'s Linda Hamilton.

She usually holds her own against whomever she finds herself cast. Smart, self-sufficient and rarely vulnerable, she is one of the new breed of screen heroines who are also portrayed by Sigourney Weaver in 1979's *Alien*. While not the most recognized name among today's leading actresses, she is in demand with producers and directors who appreciate strong, independent women and use them in their films.

The younger of two children, Carrie-Anne Moss was born in Vancouver, BC, on August 21, 1967. She was named after The Hollies' 1967 hit song *Carrie Anne*. Raised by her single mother Barbara,

Carrie-Anne displayed a gift for performing at an early age, and at age 11, she made her debut in Vancouver's Children's Musical Theatre. Later, she attended Magee, an exclusive secondary school, where one of her classmates was Gil Bellows (*Ally McBeal*). A turning point in her life came when she toured Europe with her school choir.

While abroad, she decided to become a model. At the age of 18, after working as a waitress in Vancouver, she left for Toronto to pursue her goal. Possessed of a dark, striking beauty, it wasn't long before she achieved an international reputation and was modelling in Toronto, Europe, Japan and Spain. And it was in Spain, at the age of 20, that Carrie-Anne was photographed for the first of her many international magazine covers.

While in Spain, she landed her first acting role, playing Tara McDonald on the CBS television series *Dark Justice* (1991–93),which was filmed in Barcelona. Carrie-Anne relocated to the U.S. the following year when the producers decided to switch the show's location from Spain to Los Angeles.

The move to California provided Carrie-Anne with the opportunity to learn and expand her craft. She showed herself to be a dedicated actress, playing onstage at the Hudson Theater in a production of *Outward Bound*, then later studying at the prestigious American Academy of Dramatic Arts in Pasadena.

Following graduation from AADA, Carrie-Anne began her acting career in earnest. She paid her dues playing guest roles in such TV series as *Street Justice*, *Nightmare Café*, the vampire-cop hybrid *Forever Knight*, *Silk Stalkings*, *L.A. Law*, *Baywatch* and, ironically, a show entitled *The Matrix* (which has no relation to the 1999 blockbuster). Carrie-Anne also provided voice-over work for the Spider-Man animated series.

Her most rewarding television performance came in 1996, when she played Irene Zuko in an episode of the Canadian-produced series *Due South*. For her role, she was nominated for a Gemini Award for "Best Performance by an Actress in a Guest Role in a Dramatic Series."

Her hard work brought Carrie-Anne to the attention of producer Aaron Spelling, who cast her as Carrie Spencer in his short-lived TV series *Models Inc.* (1994–95), co-starring Garcelle Beauvais.

More television roles followed. She appeared as a guest star so often that it is estimated Carrie-Anne was seen on television a total of 60 hours, not including her two series, in her first six years in the business.

Carrie-Anne also appeared in small roles in forgettable films. *The Soft Kill* (1994) was notable only because she had a topless scene. *Lethal Tender* (1997) and *The Secret Life of Algernon* are two of her other titles. With her film career going nowhere, Carrie-Anne returned to television and signed on for the role of Lucinda Scott in *F/X: The Series* (1996–97).

Then she heard about a science-fiction film getting ready to go into production called *The Matrix*.

Keanu Reeves had been cast in the lead male role, but directors Andy and Larry Wachowski had not found a suitable female co-star. Their criteria were that the female co-star must be a satisfactory counterpart to Keanu's complex character, and she must be up to the physical demands of the role. Carrie-Anne had the dark, stunning looks that perfectly complemented those of Keanu, but there were doubts regarding her athletic ability and stamina. Carrie-Anne auditioned six times for the directors before she convinced them she could handle the physical aspect of the part.

The film, shot in Australia, was a gruelling experience for all concerned, requiring endless technical experimentation and precise choreography in the fight sequences. What emerged onscreen was a visually dazzling motion picture with lots of action and a thought-provoking story line. Carrie-Anne prepared hard for the part, and it paid off. She looked sensational as the latex catsuit-clad Trinity, meeting the physical demands of her role and pairing well with her co-star onscreen—and offscreen as well.

According to reports, co-stars Keanu and Carrie-Anne dated for awhile but broke up, while still remaining friends. Carrie-Anne married that same year to actor Steven Roy.

Much to everyone's surprise, *The Matrix* (1999) became not merely a success, but a bona fide blockbuster. With the picture's release, Carrie-Anne Moss suddenly found herself a movie star. Solidifying her new status, she won a Golden State

Award for Best Actress in a Leading Role and was inundated with movie offers.

Now able to have some direction over her career, she decided to try a change-of-pace role and accepted a supporting role in the comedy *The Crew* (2000). In this film, Richard Dreyfuss, Burt Reynolds, Seymour Cassel and Dan Hedaya play four retired mobsters who decide to relive their glory days but cross a Latino drug lord who mistakenly believes they have murdered his father. Carrie-Anne plays investigating police officer Olivia Neal, who is later discovered to be Dreyfuss' long-lost daughter. The picture is lightweight entertainment and not hard to take, but it crashed at the box office.

Realizing that comedy roles are not her forte, Carrie-Anne returned to the science fiction genre that had made her famous and co-starred alongside Val Kilmer and Tom Sizemore in *Red Planet*. Spoiled by a familiar, uninvolving plot, the film has little to recommend it.

Surprisingly, a little film called *Chocolat* provided Carrie-Anne with her next big hit. *Chocolat* was an ensemble piece that featured Juliette Binoche, Lena Olin, Judy Dench, Alfred Molina and Johnny Depp. The movie tells the story of a free-spirited chocolatier (Binoche) and her daughter who arrive in a French village and how their delicious delicacies free the townspeople of their inhibitions, to the disapproval of the town's conservative leading citizen. Even though *Chocolat* was nominated for an Academy Award for Best Picture, some reviewers criticized the film for its contrivances, although Carrie-Anne was generally accorded good reviews.

Memento (2001) was another film audiences avoided, even though it was a neat little thriller about a man suffering from memory loss (Guy Pearce) who tracks down his wife's killer by writing notes on his body. Carrie-Anne played Natalie, a seductive barmaid who helps Pearce in his search.

In 2003, Carrie-Anne reprised her most famous role as Trinity again by providing her voice for the character in two episodes of *The Animatrix*. Written by *The Matrix* creators Andy and Larry Wachowski, the series of short films was intended to tell the history of the Matrix universe and of the war between man and machine. Carrie-Anne was featured in the segments "Kid's Story" (where Keanu Reeves also provided the voice of Neo) and "Detective Story."

She returned to her fetching catsuit and sunglasses for the simultaneously filmed *The Matrix Reloaded* and *The Matrix Revolutions* (2003). Both sequels were enormous audience hits, and together, the three Matrix films earned a worldwide box office total of $592 million.

Unfortunately, Carrie-Anne's next movie, the intriguing crime thriller *Suspect Zero* (2004), co-starring Oscar winner Ben Kingsley, caused no ripples at the box office.

Carrie-Anne has endured both the highs and lows of the entertainment business. She understands that there are no certainties in the industry. Despite the tremendous high points she has reached with the Matrix series, she could still quickly become unpopular and not be offered good roles. She says the best way to have a successful career is to keep working. To that end, Carrie-Anne has a number of films slated for 2005: *Sledge: The Untold Story*, *The Chumscrubber*, *Mini's First Time* and, the most exciting prospect of all, *Mission Impossible III*. There has been no talk of a fourth Matrix, but with grosses being so high for the film released so far, the Wachowski brothers may attempt to rejuvenate their successful franchise.

In the hope that she will star in another Matrix film, Carrie-Anne keeps herself in shape. Her exercise routine includes rollerblading, bicycling and "karobics," karate combined with aerobics. She currently resides in Los Angeles with her husband, actor Steven Roy. They have one child, a son born in 2003.

Regarding her role in *The Matrix*, Carrie-Anne recently said: "After the movie came out, I couldn't wear sunglasses. When I put them on, people recognized me."

CHAPTER TEN

Michael J. Fox
(1961–)

IT CAN BE SAID WITHOUT EXAGGERATION THAT MICHAEL J. Fox is Canada's most beloved star. He achieved superstar status at a young age and he has retained it, even if many of his films have not been well received by critics and the ticket-buying public. He was first successful in his native Canada. Hollywood producers recognized the quality of his work and summoned him to California.

After an initial small success in film and television, Michael found himself unemployed and broke. He was just one of many out-of-work actors struggling to find jobs. It seemed that the odds for stardom were against him. He was undersized, although not unattractive, neither was he blessed with classic movie star looks. But he came to Tinseltown with one weapon to help him defeat the odds—talent.

And it was that inherent talent mixed with an overwhelming ambition that propelled Michael J. Fox into the show business stratosphere. He is that rarity—a TV superstar who made the successful transition to motion pictures. He conquered that medium, then returned to TV where he scored

Back to the Future (1985)

another hit. This star status he would still be holding had not a strange fate set in.

Since the age of 30, Michael has struggled with Parkinson's Disease with the same courage and tenacity that had set him on the road to television and motion picture stardom. Even though the signs of his illness, perpetual movement and awkward gestures, were there, he kept it private as long as he could until he had to reveal the truth to his adoring public. Michael was forced to decrease his acting commitments and devotes most of his time and energies to help discover a cure for Parkinson's.

Michael maintains that a cure will be found within his lifetime. If researchers pursue this objective with the same perseverance and tenacity that Michael J. Fox is facing his challenge, then one can indeed feel optimistic about the outcome.

Michael J. Fox was born Michael Andrew Fox on June 9, 1961, in Edmonton, Alberta. His parents, William and Phyllis Fox, already had three children (Steven, Karen and Jackie), and another (Kelli) followed Michael.

William Fox served in the Canadian Army, so was stationed at various bases across Canada. During Michael's early years, the family lived in such locations as Chilliwack, BC and North Bay, Ontario. Often such frequent moves make it difficult for children to establish friendships, but Michael was a gregarious, outgoing boy who quickly learned to adapt to the life of an army brat and never had difficulty making friends.

When Michael was five, the Fox family settled in Burnaby, a suburb of Vancouver. In his childhood Michael was curious and inquisitive with a wide variety of interests, including a passion for music and hockey. He expressed an interest to play on a professional hockey team, but he never reached the league's height requirement so could not even try out.

Michael also had an artistic side, showing a flare for drawing. He also enjoyed participating in his school's drama class, but only as a hobby. He never gave any thought to pursuing acting as a profession, but Michael had a natural talent, and his drama instructor Ross Jones recognized it. When he heard about a new TV show called *Leo and Me* that was casting for the role of a 10-year-old boy, Jones suggested that Michael audition for the part of Jamie Romano. Even though Michael was 15 at the time, he looked younger. Mike read for the producers and won the role on the CBC series (where he was billed as "Mike Fox"). *Leo and Me* lasted only 13 weeks, but its impact on Michael was considerable.

Michael decided that he wanted to make acting his career. He became involved in local theatre productions, and in 1979 auditioned for and won a role in an American made-for-television movie that was filming in Vancouver, *Letters from Frank*. In his feature film debut, 18-year-old Michael worked with the legendary Art Carney and Maureen Stapleton, playing their grandson, Ricki.

Both Carney and Stapleton were impressed with Michael's talent and encouraged him in his acting ambitions. His performance in the film also caught the eye of Hollywood producers, and he began receiving other movie offers.

Michael discussed the offers with his parents, and they supported him in his decision to try his luck in Hollywood. A move to Hollywood at this time meant that Michael would not finish high school even though he was within weeks of that goal. But it was an exciting, once-in-a-lifetime opportunity for him. His parents' only condition was that he wait until he turned 18. Just after his birthday, William drove Michael down to Los Angeles and gave him $3000 to help him along.

Michael had one minor obstacle to overcome— his name. There was already a Michael Fox working as an actor in the industry. He didn't want to use Michael A. Fox because it might lend itself to jokes and ridicule—Michael, *a fox!*—and he wouldn't be taken seriously. As a tribute to one of his favourite actors, Michael J. Pollard, Michael decided on "J." as his middle initial.

Michael's career began on a promising note. He was awarded a small part as Scott in Disney's second PG-rated film *Midnight Madness* (1980). The film, dealing with college kids on an all-night scavenger hunt, was not an auspicious debut. It was trashed by critics and flopped at the box office.

Fortunately, Michael's next assignment was a better opportunity. He was cast as Willy-Joe Hall in the TV series *Palmerstown, U.S.A.* The show had an impressive pedigree, its creators being Norman Lear (*All in the Family*) and *Roots* author Alex Haley. Anticipations were high for its success. Even though critics applauded *Palmerstown, U.S.A.*, the show never caught on with viewers, and the series was cancelled after two seasons. The show would probably have ended sooner if not for the participation of Lear and Haley.

Even with the show's cancellation, Michael's career fared well. He regularly guest starred on many of the top-rated shows of the day, including *Family*, *Lou Grant*, *Night Court* and *Trapper John, M.D.* He also appeared in the TV movie *Trouble in the High Country*, directed by industry veteran Vincent Sherman.

Then suddenly offers of work dried up around 1981. This was a difficult period for Michael as he was $30,000 in debt. He'd been living comfortably, but was now forced to move out of his apartment suite into a garage apartment. He sold his car and subsisted on macaroni and cheese. He began selling his sectional sofa, one piece at a time.

The state of his finances depressed him, which, in turn, caused him to put on weight which, combined with his slight 1.65-metre height, made the prospect of obtaining leading roles unlikely. At that low point, he considered going back to Vancouver and giving up on his dream.

He decided to give it another shot. He got himself out of his depression, dropped the extra weight, and his luck changed.

In 1982, he appeared as Arthur in *Class of 1984*, opposite fellow Canadian Al Waxman. The film is an unpleasant story about a tough inner city school dominated by a drug-dealing psychopathic student (Timothy Van Patten) who harasses new teacher Perry King. Michael's role was small and forgettable, but at least he was back on track.

His agent told him about an audition that was being held for a yuppie, ultraconservative teenager on a new situation comedy on NBC. Michael did his read in a unique way. Instead of being polite, he came across as obnoxious as possible because that's how the character was supposed to be. The show's creator Gary David Goldberg was impressed, but NBC President Brandon Tartikoff had reservations about hiring Michael, saying his face would not have appeal on school lunch boxes. Eventually, Tartikoff relented on the advice of a casting director, and Michael was given the role of Alex P. Keaton on the show *Family Ties*.

Even though the series was cleverly written and well acted, *Family Ties* initially had a hard time finding an audience. The show's ratings that first season were so low that NBC considered cancelling it. But they decided to try it for another season, and that's when the program caught on with viewers. It was evident that it was Michael's wiseacre character that attracted the viewers. Michael never let the attention go to his head. He always made sure to praise his co-stars so their participation would not be ignored.

Michael was earning big money, and now he was more careful handling it. He knew his luck could run out at any time, and he didn't want to find himself in the same financial straits as before.

The show's viewing audience continued to grow so that by the third season the program was a hit, especially after it was placed to follow the phenomenally successful *The Cosby Show*. Michael's popularity soared. During breaks in filming, he starred in two TV movies, *High School, U.S.A.* (1983) and *Poison Ivy* (1985). Neither project enhanced Michael's career, but during the making of *Poison Ivy*, he had a brief relationship with co-star Nancy McKeon, who was starring in her own popular series *The Facts of Life* (1979–88).

The year 1985 was a good one for Michael. He was nominated for an Emmy for Best Actor for his work on *Family Ties* and starred in his first feature *Teen Wolf*—a sophomoric low-budget comedy.

But the big news began when Gary David Goldberg received a call from Steven Spielberg, asking if he could use Michael for a time travel story he was planning to produce. Goldberg explained to Spielberg that Michael was not available because of *Family Ties'* tight taping schedule. Goldberg did not tell Michael about the offer because *Family Ties* was doing so well in the ratings—because of Michael— and he didn't want to risk losing Michael to a motion picture career. Director Robert Zemekis began filming with Eric Stoltz in the role of Marty McFly. Stoltz, while a good dramatic actor, did not bring to the part the lighthearted quality it

required. Zemekis appealed to Goldberg again who agreed to let Michael make *Back to the Future* if he still did his work for the TV show.

Although Michael was thrilled, accepting the role in *Back to the Future* forced him into a dizzying, exhausting work schedule. Every day he rehearsed for *Family Ties* from 10:00 AM to 6:00 PM, then he rushed to the *Back to the Future* set where he rehearsed and then shot until 2:30 AM. Fridays were particularly rough, because they were taping days for *Family Ties*. Michael rehearsed from noon until 5:00 PM, performed two tapings, and then reported to the film set by 10:00 PM. For two months, Michael got by on four hours sleep per night. Fortunately, he'd always had an abundance of energy, but even that began to drain as the shooting progressed.

But it was worth it. *Back to the Future* was released on July 4, 1985 and became an enormous hit, remaining Number One at the box office for most of the summer and eventually earning a worldwide gross of $351 million. The film also made Michael J. Fox an overnight international superstar.

Michael now received dozens of film offers, but he made it clear that he planned to stay loyal to *Family Ties*. It was a true family set, shown by the fact that the other cast members expressed pride, not envy, concerning Michael's success. Michael said that he would not leave the show until the network canceled it—and he kept his word.

Michael was rewarded for remaining with *Family Ties* when he was presented with the Emmy Award for Best Actor in a Situation Comedy Series in 1986. To show his appreciation to the show that he admitted had made him famous, the mega-box office champ agreed to appear in a made-for-TV movie based on the series, *Family Ties Vacation*.

He kept busy with movie work when the cameras stopped rolling on the series. Unfortunately, his choice of projects did not always help his career. He played an offbeat role as rock musician Jake Resnick in the drama *Light of Day* that he probably accepted more for the opportunity to display his musical talents and play opposite real-life rocker Joan Jett than for the story itself. The movie grossed a measly amount at the box office.

The following year he appeared in *The Secret of my Success*, an apparent surefire winner that fared well at the worldwide box office. The secret to the film's success was Michael's likeable playing of his established comedic character.

The year 1987 also brought Michael his second consecutive Emmy Award for Best Actor in a Comedy Series for *Family Ties*. He later won the award a third time for that role. In addition, *Family Ties* was recognized as the second highest rated show on television.

In 1988, Michael was cast as Jamie Conway in *Bright Lights, Big City*. Acting opposite fellow Canadian Kiefer Sutherland, Michael played the challenging part of an idealistic young Midwesterner who is trapped in a kaleidoscope of drug abuse and other night life excesses. But again audiences were reluctant to accept Michael in an uncharacteristic role.

The film reunited Michael with Tracy Pollan, who had played the role of Alex's girlfriend Ellen Reed on *Family Ties*. Onscreen, their relationship was bittersweet, but in real life, a true love affair had developed between the two when they were in the series together. After being reunited on the film set, they married on July 16, 1988.

Unfortunately, Michael's popularity made it difficult for the two to enjoy the sweet, simple wedding they had hoped for. As soon as the location became public knowledge, the paparazzi swarmed in, attempting to snap photographs that could be sold for high fees to tabloids. Most got only aerial views that didn't satisfy a celebrity-hungry public. After 16 years, Michael and Tracy are still together and have four children.

Michael's film career picked up speed when *Family Ties* was nearing the end of its seven-year run. Offers of movie roles flooded in, and Michael had his pick of virtually any property. Unfortunately, his choices were rather hit-and-miss.

On the surface, the projects he chose seemed promising. The Brian De Palma-directed *Casualties of War* (1989) where Michael played Private Eriksson, a soldier with a conscience who was entrenched in the U.S.–Vietnam conflict and pitted against the merciless Sean Penn. It appeared to have strong box office potential, but audiences stayed away, perhaps offended by the movie's brutal subject matter.

Michael remained loyal to *Family Ties*, but he and fellow series regular Michael Gross once joked that the series should end with the whole Keaton clan dying in a flaming plane crash so that there would be no chance for a TV reunion years later.

After *Family Ties* ended its successful seven-year run on May 17, 1989, Michael focused his talents on a movie career. He had a good running start with the *Back to the Future* sequels, filmed simultaneously but released a year apart, in 1989 and 1990. Both films earned enormous box office takes. While *Back to the Future II* was more successful commercially, critics preferred the third film in the series, which allowed Marty McFly the opportunity to travel back to the Old West to rescue the eccentric inventor Doc Brown (Christopher Lloyd).

During the making of *Back to the Future Part II*, Michael became a father for the first time, when Tracy gave birth to son Sam Michael Fox. Sadly, during the filming of *Back to the Future Part III*, Michael's father William passed away. Michael had always enjoyed a close relationship with his parents and siblings, and his father's death was a devastating blow.

Following the *Back to the Future* sequels, Michael experienced professional difficulties as his box office started to falter. A promising teaming with James Woods in *The Hard Way* (1991) proved financially disappointing. In the film, Michael played spoiled movie star Nick Lang who tags along with Woods, a tough New York City cop, to

Back to the Future (1985)

research an upcoming film role. It was an interesting concept that didn't click with moviegoers.

In *Doc Hollywood*, Michael played Dr. Benjamin Stone, a Beverly Hills plastic surgeon who has to perform community service work in rural South Carolina after a car crash. The film earned a respectable box office gross. It was during the filming of *Doc Hollywood* that Michael first noticed an uncontrollable trembling in his left small finger. As his condition worsened, Michael consulted a specialist who diagnosed Michael with Parkinson's Disease, a degenerative neurological illness that generally affects only the elderly.

Michael, distressed by this diagnosis, chose to keep the news from his public as long as possible. He began taking medication and doing light exercises to curb the symptoms. Tracy was devastated by the news but was supportive of Michael.

The movie roles kept coming, though they were a motley bunch. Michael lent his talents to such forgettable movies as *Life with Mikey* (1993) and *Greedy* (1994). Outside of Michael's energetic performance, *For Love or Money* (formerly *The Concierge*) was a forgettable comedy and proved to be another box office disappointment. His voice-over as Chance the bulldog pup in the remake of the Disney classic *Homeward Bound: The Incredible Journey* provided Michael with an impressive box office coup. In 1994 he co-starred with Woody Allen in *Don't Drink the Water*, which was Allen's TV acting and directing debut.

Overall, it was a professionally discouraging time for Michael. He saw that most of his films lacked the box office zest of his earlier ones. He tried his hand at directing an episode of HBO's *Tales from the Crypt* . In 1995, he co-produced and played a bit role in the black comedy *Coldblooded*, starring Jason Priestley as a mob bookkeeper who becomes a hit man.

The year 1995 was also significant for Michael because it was that year the high school dropout earned his GED and thus finally got his high school diploma. David Letterman, on his late night program, congratulated Michael for this achievement by presenting him with a new car.

That same year Michael's acting career seemed to be back on track when he accepted the supporting role of Lewis Rothschild, the President's chief speechwriter, in *The American President* (1995). Starring Michael Douglas, Annette Bening and Martin Sheen, the Rob Reiner-directed movie proved enormously popular with audiences.

Unfortunately, the same could not be said for the New Zealand horror film called *The Frighteners* (1996). In the picture, Michael played Frank Bannister, a psychic investigator tracking down a supernatural killer. This role was a change of pace for Michael, but unfortunately, neither his acting nor the often-grisly special effects drew in an audience.

He did another "genre" picture, this one directed by the brilliant Tim Burton. In *Mars Attacks!*, based on the controversial Topps trading cards, Michael played the egocentric newsman Jason Stone who meets his demise shortly after the aliens arrive. This film boasted impressive computer-generated special effects (including the skull-headed Martians themselves) and an all-star cast including Jack Nicholson (in a dual role), Glenn Close, Pierce Brosnan and Rod Steiger. But *Mars Attacks!* fell far short of box office expectations, considering the cost of the movie.

It seemed the one medium where Michael could not fail was television. Unlike some other movie stars, Michael was willing to appear in commercials and go on talk shows.

Then in March 1996, *Family Ties* creator Gary David Goldberg approached him about a return to series television. The show he proposed was called *Spin City*, and it was an immediate hit with viewers and critics alike. On the series he portrayed Michael "Mike" Flaherty, Deputy Mayor of New York City. Michael enjoyed playing the role. To cover his illness during the filming, he often had to put his hands in his pockets so that viewers would not see them trembling. He was happy to have the stability of a weekly television series that did not involve lengthy shooting on location away from his family. This became important to him when on February 15, 1996, Tracy gave birth to twin daughters Aquinnah Kathleen and Schuyler Frances.

It was during this pinnacle of professional and personal success that Michael divulged to the world that he was suffering from Parkinson's. He had undergone risky experimental brain surgery to slow the progress of the disease, but it was only partially successful, and his symptoms were becoming impossible to hide.

In 2000, after three successful seasons on *Spin City*, his condition made it too difficult for him to keep up with the demands of the weekly series. Charlie Sheen replaced him, although he agreed to make occasional guest appearances and remained the show's executive producer.

Once he revealed that he was suffering from Parkinson's, he received support from all over the world. Michael's announcement was intended to educate others about the ordeal of those living with Parkinson's. Among those afflicted with this neurological disorder was the late acting legend Katharine Hepburn and heavyweight boxing champion Muhammad Ali.

Michael became active in the cause to defeat Parkinson's. He hoped that his celebrity status would increase awareness and raise needed dollars to find a cure. To that end, he established The Michael J. Fox Foundation for Parkinson's Disease Research. On September 28, 1999, Michael stepped up his crusade by appearing before the U.S. Senate Appropriations Subcommittee to appeal for greater funding for Parkinson's research.

Michael still continues to act, although more frequently in roles where he is heard but not seen. He provided the voice of *Stuart Little* (1999), a charming animated story about a mouse adopted by a human family. The film was a runaway hit. The film's popularity led to a sequel three years later.

Michael supplied the voice of Stuart for the equally successful *Stuart Little 2*.

Michael also voiced Milo for the Disney animated feature *Atlantis: The Lost Empire* (2001). He is signed up to supply the vocals for the character of Marcel Maggot for the upcoming animated television movie *The Magic Seven*.

Michael's autobiography, *Lucky Man: A Memoir*, was released in bookstores on April 2, 2002. In the book Michael talks candidly about living with Parkinson's. Profits from the sale of the book go to the foundation.

In his mid-40s, Michael J. Fox has led a full life. He's experienced personal and professional highs and lows but maintains an optimistic outlook. Although he does not work at his beloved acting as much as he once did, he assures his fans that he is not going away.

Notes on Sources

Fox, Michael J. *Lucky Man: A Memoir*. New York: Hyperion, 2002.

IMDB (International Movie Data Base)

Johnston, Sheila. *Keanu*. London: Sidgwick & Jackson, 1996.

Knelman, Martin. *The Joker is Wild*. New York: Firefly Books, 2002.

Robb, Brian J. *Keanu Reeves: An Excellent Adventure*. New Jersey: Plexus Publishing, 2003.

The National Enquirer. Pam. The Life and Loves of Pamela Anderson. California: AMI Books, 2003.

Tyrell, Denise. *Brendan Fraser*. New York: Romance Foretold, 2001.